HOW TO SUCCEED IN REAL LIFE
NO MATTER WHERE YOU LAND

THE GAME OF LIFE

HOW TO SUCCEED IN REAL LIFE
NO MATTER WHERE YOU LAND

BY LOU HARRY

RUNNING PRESS
PHILADELPHIA · LONDON

9   8   7   6   5   4   3   2   1
Digit on the right indicates the number of this printing

Library of Congress Control Number: 2002108928

ISBN 0-7624-1445-6

Cover design by Whitney Cookman
Interior design by Matthew Goodman
Edited by Andra Serlin
Typography: Agenda, Formata, Din-Black, and Slimbach.
This book may be ordered by mail from the publisher.
Please include $2.50 for postage and handling.
But try your bookstore first!

Running Press Book Publishers
125 South Twenty-second Street
Philadelphia, Pennsylvania 19103-4399

Visit us on the web!
www.runningpress.com

DEDICATION

This one is for two teachers, Fred DeSantis (3rd grade) and Sue German (high school sophomore English) who delivered the message that it was okay to both think and feel.

ACKNOWLEDGEMENTS

For support, advice, and counsel during the writing of this book, I owe massive debt to Sam Stall, Emily Harry, Todd Tobias, and Rabbi Eric Bram. To Cindy Harry for a partnership in life and on this manuscript. And to Frank Kalafski and the kids of Wildwood Avenue who played board games with me.

Table of Contents

• Start college • Scholarship! • Buy books and supplies • Make new friends • Part-time job • Study for exams • Study abroad • Spring Break! • Dean's List! • Write term paper • Graduation day! • Job search/Career choice

CHAPTER 1

COLLEGE PATH
15

• Start career • Rent apartment • Raffle prize/Inheritance • Pay day 1 • Adopt a pet • Lost! • Birthday Party! • Ski accident • Win marathon! • Say no to drugs/Visit a Museum • Cycle to work/ Don't drink and drive • Flat tire

CHAPTER 2

CAREER PATH
31

• Get married • Wedding reception • Happy honeymoon! • Buy furniture/Upgrade computer • Car accident • Special Section 1: Life Quotes • Move across the country/Attend high-tech seminar • Night school 1 • Taxes due • Win lottery! • Visit in-laws • Buy a house • Pay day 2

• "You're fired!"/Lose your job • Baby boy! • Furnish baby room • Baby girl! • Win talent show! • Pay day 3 • Twins! • Box seats at the world series/50-yard-line seats at the big game • Attend Hollywood movie premiere • House flooded! • Buy big screen TV/Buy high-definition TV • Stock market soars! • Family picnic • Visit Mount Rushmore • Car stolen

CHAPTER 5

RIGHT FORK
89

• Family physicals • Tree falls on house • Return lost wallet • Run for mayor • Vote! • Tropical vacation/Buy luxury cruise online • Night school 2 • Learn CPR • Special Section 2: Life Story • Art auction • Help out at Special Olympics/Volunteer at charity event • Win Beautiful Baby contest/ Win photography contest

• Taxes due • Tennis camp • African safari/Donate computer network • Stock market crash 1 • Be my Valentine • Day care • Write best-seller • Adopt twins • Invest in Broadway play • Join health club • Family portrait • Buy sports car/Buy sport utility vehicle • Tax refund

CHAPTER 6

LEFT FORK
103

• Host Police Charity Ball • Find buried treasure!
• Donate to Art Institute • Recycle • TV game show winner! • Summer school • Have a Family Game Night™
• Learn sign language • Special Section 3: More Life Quotes • Buy lakeside cabin • Burglar! • Win Nobel Prize • Buy home gym • Stock market crash 2
• Tornado tilts house! • Moo-shu flu attack!/Life-saving operation • Buy sailboat • Sponsor golf tournament
• Mid-life crisis

CHAPTER 7

RIGHT FORK
119

• Produce rock video/Host online concert • Help the homeless
• Have tattoos removed/Have cosmetic surgery • College (for child) • Visit war memorial • Sponsor art exhibit • Grand Canyon vacation • Go fishing • Hire jockey for your racehorse
• Go hiking! • Plant a tree • Support wildlife fund • Tour Europe/Have website designed • You're a grandparent! • Pay Day 4 • Throw party for entertainment award winners
• Luxury cruise/Invest in e-commerce company • Pension
• Retire • Countryside Acres and Millionaire Estates

CHAPTER 8

MILLIONAIRE ESTATES
141

INTRODUCTION

Since first looking up at the stars and down into the faces of children, humans have been searching for the meaning of life.

And since 1959, some of these same people have been playing THE GAME OF LIFE board game.

While traveling on a road that included optional college, a mandatory wedding, and a lifetime of ups and downs, the game involved packing your car with little peg babies, deciding whether to invest in the stock market, and, if you spun the big wheel well, landing a permanent parking spot at Millionaire Estates. With one foot in fantasy and one in reality, THE GAME OF LIFE board game always had an element of Brady-Bunchness about it. Its experiences were recognizable but heightened, reality-based but simplified. My family never experienced a tornado, but we did have some minor flooding. Pay day wasn't quite as grand, but the checks did arrive. And while we never visited Mount Rushmore, we did make it to the Baseball Hall of Fame.

Unlike real life, though, each adventure on THE GAME OF LIFE board was self-contained. Each spin, a new beginning. You were always heading in the right direction, no matter which fork in the road you chose. And if you happened to get too far ahead, spaces on the board made you wait for your fellow players. It was okay to win, but not to blow your opponent away.

Of the closetful of diversions I played when I was a kid, THE GAME OF LIFE board game is one of the few my own kids play. It has few peers among representational games (as opposed to abstract games like Parcheesi® and Sorry®). Sure, there's Monopoly®—and if you are being generous you might add Clue®, Careers® and Risk®—but while those games require a sense of strategy more likely to engage the ten-and-up crowd, this game has across-the-board appeal.

Unlike most board games, THE GAME OF LIFE never seemed to really be about acquiring money, making conquests, or beating another player to a goal. It always seemed less about winning and more about, well, living. The fun came from making the initial decision of college vs. going directly into business. It came from seeing how many pink or blue kids ended up in your sporty little playing-piece car. It came from heading over those plastic mountains, getting a sense that you were collecting a full life, and eventually retiring at the natural end of the game (heck, even if you were the first to the end of the board, you weren't necessarily the winner). Sometimes, when my friends and I played as kids, we didn't even bother adding up our cash at the end.

To be sure, THE GAME OF LIFE board game wasn't entirely paved with happiness. There were some setback spaces. The stock market slumped. You were robbed. Taxes came due. But the game never became realistic to a fault. No one died. There was a car accident space but no injuries (except perhaps when our dog knocked over the game board). Charity was something you gave to, not something you received. It was never too difficult to get rid of your promissory-note debt. The majority of players ended the game with a nice bankroll. You never really felt like you were against the other players—not like the dog-eat-dog world of other board games. Here there was nothing you could do to seriously hurt another player's chances. You just did the best you could for yourself and, if you felt like it, did the math at the end.

We didn't play the game to learn life lessons. We played for the fun of it. But, in hindsight—and as I watch my kids play with the same gusto I did—an underlying message emerges.

The ages of man are connected, the game seems to be saying. As you grow up, you will experience life from different perspectives. You will take your turn stepping out of the nest. You will be the person at the altar. You will be the homebuyer, the insurance-owner, the parent. And you—yes, you—will eventually retire.

You are on a journey and it doesn't go backwards.

As such, I found that THE GAME OF LIFE board game is not just a fun diversion, it's also a great springboard for contemplating the events, large and small, that make up a full life. In the pages that follow, I've taken just about every space on the board and used it as a launching point to discuss how we experience the real world. What questions does this particular life event raise? What are some healthy questions to ask yourself as you anticipate that life moment? Some of the discussion is practical, some whimsical, some emotional, and some philosophical. Mixed into these chapters, you'll also find collections of quotes about life from Charlie Brown to Albert Einstein as well as a brief history of the game itself.

While you may not have played the board game in years, my hope is that this book nudges you into thinking about the world with the same openness that you did as a child. I hope that, as we linger on each space, you are inspired to look at the life ahead of you or the life you've lived thus far. It is my intent to provide a fun framework to some serious thought and a serious framework for some fun thought.

To butcher a line from Shakespeare's *Twelfth Night:* If life is a game, play on.

THE SPACES

On THE GAME OF LIFE board, each space is an individual action, with little or no bearing on what has happened before or after. In real life, though, individual events don't exist in a vacuum.

In the pages that follow, I've taken a trip around THE GAME OF LIFE board, using each space to explore the real issues behind the life situation on each square.

If some of the squares don't seem familiar to you, it could be because you've played an earlier edition of the game. In some cases, I've stuck with older versions. In others, I've used the updates. And if you don't see as many Pay Days as you remember, don't despair. I've kept only four to represent distinct moments in your working life.

As with the game itself, I expect you'll skip some spaces as you read this book. Find the ones that make sense for you—or just spin the spinner and work your way through. While I can't promise that you'll arrive at Millionaire Estates a wealthy person, I can echo Aristotle who said, "an unexamined life is not worth living."

START

The GAME OF LIFE board game skips the first 18 or so years of our existence, and, instead, begins when most people are making their first major decisions independent of parents.

But does life really begin at 18? There are those who finish high school clinging to the glory of youth and suggesting that there is no real life after high school—that the best of life happens there and the rest is downhill. These folks thrived on the safety of high school: the rigid class schedules, class hierarchy, and closed universe of faculty and students (plus perhaps the relative ease of making it onto the football team or into the school play). The world beyond doesn't offer such simplicity or such clear-cut rules and these people find it almost impossible to navigate. You can find some of these folks hanging out near convenience stores. Others appear to outward eyes to be successful, but secretly yearn for days gone by.

For others, high school graduation is just the starting point. What happened before isn't terribly relevant to them. Who can blame them for a "Don't Look Back" approach when you think of all the embarrassing incidents? After all, this is where you stumbled through puberty, where people know you not just as who you are now, but also as the awkward adolescent and the uncouth kid.

The reality, of course, is that we are constantly faced with ways to reinvent ourselves. But that reinvention always brings with it qualities from the person we've been. And that's true whether we are just leaving high school, just leaving college, about to get married, or facing the prospect of parenthood (or grandparenthood).

So start now…

COLLEGE PATH

START COLLEGE
Borrow
$40,000

At the beginning of THE GAME OF LIFE board game, there's a choice to be made—one of the few decisions you really have to make in the game. Do you pursue a degree in higher education or head right to the school of hard knocks? Here, it's a gamble you make based on whether you prioritize getting into the money-making world more quickly, or if you prefer to invest a little to reap larger rewards in the long run. In real life, though, such decisions are often made based on economic status, family values, and how well you managed high school.

THE GAME OF LIFE board game, being an optimistic game (at least in the revised version, where ending up in the Poor House is not an option), does not allow for any variations from these two paths. For example, you can't change schools three times, switch majors four times, and ultimately drop out, deep in student loan debt and without a degree. You also can't go straight into business, find nothing but minimum wage jobs and eventually turn to a life of crime.

So let's say you take the road to college. Considering the cost of college these days, $40,000 starts to seem conservative—and, of course, that's not counting books, housing and the massive credit card debt that students today are racking up.

The problem with graduating as a heavy debtor is that it limits your liberty. Want to move to the big city and pursue your dream career? Well, unless you have a financially supportive family, you might find yourself working that dream job and a second job, too. Want to take time to find yourself? That's great in theory, but may lead to you defaulting on your loans. If you've still got time, remember that debt curtails your freedom. Ask yourself if that stack of CDs, the new clothes, and the nightly dining out are really worth it.

The goal: Graduate with the education you want, but also with your debt in check.

SCHOLARSHIP!
Collect
$20,000

Score!

You've hit the academic lottery. But this one isn't based on luck. It's based on the hard work you put forth in high school. Or a special area of talent you've mastered. Hustling for whatever scholarships you can is not only practical, it's a good way to distance yourself from your parents' purse strings. There are books out there that contain pages and pages of untapped, no-one-ever-thought-to-apply-for funds—check them out. You'd be surprised what money you may qualify for just because you're Jewish, of Armenian descent, have relatives in the military, or once played the trumpet.

Once you've been awarded a scholarship, don't forget where the money came from. Send thank you notes not only when you recieve the check, but also when you graduate. Decide to be the kind of person who appreciates what is given.

BUY BOOKS AND SUPPLIES
Pay
$5000

Chances are you've never paid $200 for a book. Chances are you can't imagine any book short of an original manuscript of The Bible signed by the authors being *worth* $200. But that's the kind of cash outlay you'll have to make as a college student—and you have no choice in the matter. (It's even more frustrating when your professor is the author and you know that he knows that no one in his or her right mind would buy the book if it wasn't mandatory.)

Most of these books you'll sell back at the end of the semester. Some you'll cling to, convincing yourself that you'll actually use *Criminology in the 18th Century* as a reference in years to come. The reality is, you won't. But having those books around may still be helpful, acting as a tangible reminder of the time you spent in classes. Later on in your college career when you are trying your best to find motivation, open up a textbook from your freshman year and see how simple it seems now. You've certainly come a long way. You should be proud. Now go study for your Modern Africa exam. Go!

MAKE NEW FRIENDS

Unless you are a military brat or in the witness protection program, you probably spent all of your high school years in one, or maybe two, places, and you made friends based on the pool of people you lived near. Upon hitting college you'll soon realize that even the most diverse high school populations don't begin to touch the range of people you'll meet at even an average university.

One of the most important things you can do during your college years is to meet people and make connections. From your freshman dorm roommate to the looker in your Comparative Literature course, new friendship opportunities are plentiful in college. Take advantage of this time before you enter the "real world." Unless you are a commuter, you live with these people. You eat meals with these people. You party with these people. They see you at your best and worst. At least some of them will be as succesful as you'd like to be. They can become your network when you graduate. So choose wisely. The people who've got it going on—not materially, but intellectually, spiritually, and humanely—are good people to meet.

An old Girl Scout song says, "Make new friends and keep the old. One is silver and the other's gold." Truth is, though, that many of those people who signed your high school yearbook with the acronym RMA (Remember Me Always) won't be creating new memories with you. Some stay close. Others are on the sending or receiving ends of occasional e-mails. Most fade away, to be embraced at your ten-year reunion. This is not an insult to those friendships. It's simply that, as the years go by, you meet more and more people. Some of them you'll want to spend time with. Given that there are only so many hours in the day, there are a limited amount of friendships you can actively maintain without trivializing the value of your closest ones. Learn to value good acquaintances as well as good friends.

The challenge is not to feel guilty as the time period between contact grows. Your relationships make up the person you become. As you grow, your needs change. It's okay for people to come in and out of your life. Just be sure to keep the keepers.

PART-TIME JOB
Collect
$5000

A part-time job is ripe for drudgery. But it's also an opportunity to pick up a little dough while satisfying a part of yourself that isn't concerned with career advancement. That could mean working in a bookstore. Serving coffee. Doing yard work. Waiting tables at a place where desirable dates may be found. Whatever the case, seize the moment, but make sure you keep in mind the "why," not just the "how much am I being paid."

There are four main reasons to pick up a part-time job:

1. You need the bucks. This is probably the primary reason that you are spending your time behind the register at Starbucks rather than in your pajamas in your dorm room/apartment.

2. You want the perks. The caffeine discount you could get by working at the aforementioned Starbucks may help you get through many an all-night study session for your Physiology 101 class. The movie theater ushering job lets you see all those flicks you would have paid for otherwise (and, let's be honest, it's an easy gig: When was the last time you saw an usher actually do anything?). And the gig in the radio station's promotions department certainly helps your CD collection. Factor in these nonmonitary perks when you weigh one potential part-time job against another.

3. You want to learn a new skill set. Whether to help transition you to a better gig or to have a fallback in case you lose your main job later on in life, this isn't a bad idea. From managing the breakfast shift at a fast-food joint to taking some temp work in the corporate world, these

skills and connections could come in handy later.

4. You can't think of anything you'd rather do with the time, so you might as well get paid for it. This is the worst excuse of the bunch. If this is, in fact, the case, think about studying more. If you're already at the head of the class, try taking tougher classes. Okay, Scholar, if you really don't need the money and you are acing the toughest courses available, why not volunteer for a worthwhile endeavor? Greenpeace, your local food bank, or a promising-but-underfunded political candidate could sure use you. And, let's face it—volunteer work looks great on a resume.

Speaking of resumes, if you haven't gotten enough professional experience in your field to fill out a one-pager, part-time work can certainly help. Editors look for journalists who have spent time with other publications. Sales positions are certainly more attainable when the applicant has shown an ability to work in that high-pressure environment. Your resume is the answer to the question: What have *you* done that the rest of the stack hasn't? A part-time job can make the difference.

STUDY FOR EXAMS
LOSE NEXT TURN

Educators will tell you that if you've done what you were supposed to have done and studied all semester, cramming for exams shouldn't be necessary. By the end of the term, you either know the material or you don't. But the reality is that if there's an important test on Tuesday, then you're probably going to be up late getting ready for it on Monday (assuming, of course, that you care about your grades).

When you do find yourself with the need to cram, keep in mind these late-night study tips:

* Study with folks who actually know what they're doing. Being the most knowledgeable person in the room won't help you here.

* Don't study on your bed. It's too easy to go to sleep. Instead, find a comfortable, but not sleep-inducing, area to set up camp. The dorm lounge is a good choice if you don't get too distracted. Perhaps your campus library is open all night?

* Never underestimate the power of a yellow highlighter. But use it judiciously. Turning whole pages of text yellow is counterproductive.

A valuable skill you can learn to apply here—and carry over to situations later in life—is the understanding that not everyone is on the same stress curve that you are. A crazy day for you may be a relatively easy one for someone else. But it's normal, when you are under the gun, to think the rest of the world should be as well. And when you see others doing what you perceive as "chilling out," it's easy to get short with them. On the other hand, when you're in a low-key mode, without deadlines on the immediate horizon, words like "relax" and "take it light" come easy, and you could easily come across as an insensitive slacker.

When in a work environment, it's never a good idea to be too far on either extreme. Look swamped too often and you'll appear disorganized and not up to the job. Look too low-key and people might wonder why you are collecting a paycheck.

And when the big project is due at the office, remember the skills you trial-and-errored back in college. Think about that all-night study session and the good grade that came out of it. Remind yourself that you were hired for a reason. You can get the job done. You passed that exam; you'll get through this.

STUDY ABROAD

There will be plenty of reasons to talk yourself out of taking a semester abroad. You'll be leaving behind friends who you are only going to be with for a short time anyway. Perhaps there's a romantic relationship that is likely to be destroyed by foreign encounters (absence may make the heart grow fonder, but there's also the old "out of sight, out of mind" axiom). You may have to miss out on favorite extra-curricular activities (the Peking campus probably doesn't have a football team). And it's guaranteed that your friends will mock your new accent when you return.

But for every reason *not* to go there's a continent full of reasons *to* go. The experience of simply living among people of another culture is growth enhancing. You'll expand your sense of the world while learning about who you are. You'll have the opportunity to redefine yourself in another context, to create a new identity amongst people who do not know you (but, that doesn't mean pulling a *Talented Mr. Ripley* move).

If you are so inclined, you can truly learn another language—something very difficult to do stateside with just a few courses behind you. If you are studying in France, challenge yourself to only speak French when you do your shopping. Don't just hang out with fellow Americans—you could be doing that in Cleveland. Speaking a foreign language looks great on a resume and can open up many a career door—just remember to stay in practice between your trip and your job search.

SPRING BREAK!
Pay
$5000

You know what you are getting into. Don't pretend you don't. The rituals of Spring Break are no secret. Not to you. Not to your parents. Not to the police who may well be standing over you as you call your parents.

There will be alcohol. There will be members of the opposite sex looking for fast-forward encounters. There will be moneymakers trying to maximize the amount you spend and the amount of exposure you get to their products. There will be the hot sun of day and the crowded clubs and hotel rooms at night. And, no matter how bizarre things get, you will know that you will be back to school in a few days.

That knowledge can be your best friend or your worst enemy. As your friend, it can remind you that you aren't in some alternate reality. This is the real world and whatever you do, you have to take that into account when you consider what kind of person you are.

As the devil on your shoulder, though, it can keep reminding you that your time on this vacation is finite, that such revelry is unlikely to happen for you again...possibly ever. And it can help convince you to do things you would not think of doing otherwise.

If you decide to exercise a little restraint, you can always do what most other college students do when recounting stories of Spring Break: **Lie**.

DEAN'S LIST!

You've made the grade. At least by your school's standards. What that means, though, depends on how tough your school is, how tough your program is, and how much leeway your teachers gave you. Nevertheless, be proud. For sure, being on the dean's list impresses the parental units and perhaps scores some additional spending money for next semester.

So who is this Dean person? And is he or she someone you should actually get to know? Why not take advantage of your position on this list and drop the Dean a note. It may sound like pandering, but it's actually a smart opportunity to make some connections. While there's a rich history of antagonism toward college deans that can be traced back through *Animal House* and other movie comedies to the '60s protest movement, there is actually a good chance that your dean is a community leader who could be very helpful when the job search begins (or when the party you're throwing gets busted by campus police).

Slightly off topic, but you might have already realized that some spaces on THE GAME OF LIFE board have exclamation points in them. Generally, when you see an exclamation point, you are about to collect money—but you are also about to do it for something that is not totally within your control. In this case, your appearance on the Dean's List does reflect your academic stature, but it is also influenced by the performance of others in your class. As with most achievements in life, there is that outside-of-yourself factor in which your fate depends not just on what you do, but on what others do as well. This shouldn't keep you from giving everything you've got, but it should keep you at least a little bit humble.

WRITE TERM PAPER

After college, it is unlikely that you will ever again have the opportunity to write down everything you know about a given topic. You may never even be asked to expound on any topic of substance. How many waiters get requests to go on at length about the art of the eighteenth century? How many CEOs have a vehicle through which to expound on the physics of billiards?

But in college you get to write about all sorts of things, from "The Movie *Groundhog Day* Through the Eyes of Eastern Religions", to "The Economics of the Death Penalty", or "Benjamin and William Henry Harrison: A Study in Contrasts." A few years out of a university setting, the subjects may seem absurdly arcane and even trivial, but the point isn't so much to make you an expert on the obscure. Rather, it's about teaching you to focus, to research, and to articulate.

The first question is: Are you going to write the paper yourself? The answer is of course you are. You won't be one of those students who opt to simply buy a term paper. The advent of the Internet has made shopping for a term paper easier than ever. Remember, though: the Internet has also made spotting a fake term paper easier than ever. And if you do consider turning in bogus work, you should ask yourself this question: What am I doing at college, and why am I paying all this dough if I'm that averse to doing the work?

Next issue: Picking the right topic for your paper. In most cases, term paper topics aren't assigned, but they *are* approved. Do you find something that you know the professor is an expert in? If you do, you could endear yourself to him or her with your shared interest, or it could backfire and invite closer scrutiny. Then again, if a subject comes across as fringe, so could you. Your term paper may not be your life's work, but it will take up a good chunk of your time. Make sure you have at least a passing interest in the topic.

The big step comes when the research begins. This is as much a skill to be learned as it is a means to an end. Improving your ability to find and process the material you need is an achievement as valuable in the long run as any set of facts you are likely to memorize. Remember: the librarian is there to help you. He or she may even be insulted if you don't come begging for help. So make a librarian's day: ask questions.

Then there's the writing—probably the first time you've tackled a prose project this extensive. You need to structure the piece, hold the reader's attention, and not make spelling and grammatical errors that make you look like anything but the scholar that you are.

Finally, ask for another set of eyes. After you've gone through the obvious computer spell check, turn the manuscript over to a friend (preferably a very anal friend) to critique. Then give the paper a read out loud. You'll be amazed at how many awkward stretches you encounter. When those corrections are folded in, run spell check again. And remember, perfection ain't perfection if it's not turned in on time.

GRADUATION DAY!

It's done. Well, technically it was done when you took your last exam. But now it's official and you're going to be handed a degree and move your tassel from one side of your mortar board to the other. (Which way is that exactly? Like the difference between stalactites and stalagmites, it's always hard to remember.)

Expect seriously mixed emotions during all of this. Why did you waste time in that trendy film studies course? Why didn't you play more? Why didn't you work harder? Why didn't you have the guts to take things beyond the flirting stage with that cutie in Advanced Chemistry?

You'll be reminded in subtle and obvious ways that you are not just graduating from college, you are graduating from the universe of people you've gotten to know—probably the first people you've really connected with independent of your home town and your family ties.

The "real world" awaits. You no longer have the cushion of the ivy walls (or dandelion walls depending on where you went to school) to hide behind. The "real world" doesn't grade on a curve and it won't help you to your dorm room after a rough night.

Still, this is a cause for celebration. Remember the trepidation you had as high school came to a close. It seemed like the world beyond those walls was the great unknown. Now you know a part of it. And you know that you can do just fine in the next phase of your life.

Congratulations.

JOB SEARCH/CAREER CHOICE

In a sense, you've been searching for a job and considering careers since the first time you picked up a hammer as an infant or tried to apply makeup to Barbie's tiny face with a very large lipstick. You've been on the job search since realizing that you didn't have the money to pay for the candy you wanted and began scheming how to get it. Every year that has gone by has served to either narrow or expand your focus regarding your possibilities, whether you were conscious of it or not. So you've realized that becoming a cowboy is very impractical, and there aren't many jobs that involve lying on the couch watching TV all day. So what do you want to be?

Some of the narrowing down has been taken care of already. If you opted not to study foreign languages, chances are you aren't going to be a translator. If you haven't taken the necessary pre-med courses, your odds of becoming a doctor are slim. On the other hand, by taking an intro graphic design class, your eyes may have been opened to possible careers in advertising or creating fancy-schmanzy websites.

If you haven't already taken care of job hunting during senior year, you've got to make up for lost time and get your resume out there. In theory, the resume is a document as individual as a fingerprint. It tells how you differ from everyone else in the application pile. Resist the urge to lie, or even exaggerate. If you want the gig bad enough, find a way to convince them that you are right for the job, rather than prove, by falsifying your life, that you are not. Besides, if you do land the job, you will be found out quickly if you claim to have a skill that you really don't.

Yes, it can be a Catch 22 situation: you need experience to get the job you want but can't get the job unless you have the experience. Therefore, do not underestimate the power of the internship. Yes, they offer little or no money so you may need another source of income. But if you can find a way to swing it financially and swallow your pride a bit, working as an assistant (read: gopher) can be a foot in the door in an otherwise difficult to penetrate world—and you'll make valuable contacts, too.

CAREER PATH

START CAREER

Okay, you're employed. And this isn't just some by-the-hour job. Now your salary is discussed in annual terms. And you're ready to walk in for day one.

Don't underestimate the power of first impressions. The people who interviewed you have already sized you up and, by giving you the job, have deemed you worthy to be in their midst. But the rest of the crew is already speculating about who you are and how you'll fit in. Give yourself time to work up to speed. Keep your eyes open and get a sense of office politics. Understand clearly what is expected of you. Exceed those expectations.

Other advice for day one of your job:

1. Dress appropriately, whatever that means to the particular job. If possible, get someone who actually works in whatever field you are exploring to approve your outfit (your peers are of little help here).

2. Make a real effort to learn the names of your superiors and co-workers quickly.

3. If people are going out to lunch and invite you—accept. Even if you have to order the cheapest thing on the menu, it's good to come across as social and accepting. But if gossip or superior-bashing is the order of the day, don't play along.

4. Don't make personal phone calls on company time.

5. Do personalize your space with office-appropriate pictures, knick-knacks, etc. of family and friends (if this is allowable by company policy). This announces ownership of your work area from the get-go and gives the impression that you are going to stay awhile.

6. Remind yourself on the way to work why you were offered the job and why you accepted it. Don't fall into the belief that the company owes you a living and, conversely, don't buy into the idea that you're invisible. Apart from sleeping, this is what you are going to be doing for most of your time. In fact, as an ad for a job search website points out, you'll spend more time at your job than with your family and friends. Make the most of it.

RENT APARTMENT

Pay
$5000

Why $5000? Think first and last month's rent, security deposit, a bed, home essentials, the first refrigerator full of food, etc. It's not an easy financial transition if this is your initial foray into being self-sustaining.

Your first solo apartment is not the place you'll spend the rest of your days, but it is the first place that you will be totally responsible for creating. Does that mean a beer-can pyramid or framed art gallery prints? A dishwasher emptied every morning or a sink full of bowls caked with last week's Ramen noodles?

No matter which, it's your space, and you have to decide what you are going to do with it.

Which drawer will be the one for the silverware?

How much time will you let go between changing the sheets? Just how many showers can one towel be used for before it needs washing?

Do you really need window treatments? Are you going to use milk crates as furniture? What's your toilet-paper preference: over or under? Does the trash get emptied from small trashcans to big on a daily basis, only when filled, or only when overflowing?

If you are living with a roommate, a whole different set of issues arises, including:

Whose name is the phone bill going to be in?

Pets: Yes or No? (Decide early, because one of you is going, at some point, to bring home a stray if the matter hasn't been talked about.)

If one of you goes away for a few weeks, are you both still equally responsible for the utility bills?

Drinking out of cartons: Okay, or only when the other roommate isn't around? (You know you're going to do it.)

What foods are public domain?

How many times a month—if at all—can a boyfriend or girlfriend stay over without having to pay a share of the rent?

What is the statute of limitations before you are allowed to fool around with your roommate's ex?

Living on your own certainly increases your privacy, but it can also accentuate loneliness. Are you going to use that downtime to read the books you always wanted time to conquer, create an exercise regime to increase the chance of a long and happy life, or use the time to watch every episode of *E! True Hollywood Story*?

RAFFLE PRIZE!/ INHERITANCE
Collect
$10,000

Depending on the version of THE GAME OF LIFE board game you have, this space is labeled either Raffle Prize or Inheritance. Both signal a significant unearned one-time income.

As for the raffle win, dumb luck is a part of life. Just as there's no predicting if a drunk driver is going to slam into your Honda, there's also no way of knowing if your lottery number or raffle ticket is going to bring home the big prize. The difference between the two examples, though, is that one is involuntary, while the other is elective—meaning that by buying a ticket, you are investing in the *possibility* that you are the odds-beater who will take home the prize.

When it comes to the lottery, you could spend a small fortune (or a large one) trying to be this winner. Buying a raffle ticket is a little different in that there's usually a charity involved (one that goes beyond helping a state government desperately try to balance its budget on the backs of get-rich-quickers). Buying a raffle ticket from a high school band member knocking on your door or a Rotarian trying to raise money for scholarships is an act of kindness, of charity. The chance of winning is just a way to rationalize the gift.

Didn't win this time? Keep in mind that many charities that sponsor raffles brag about the fact that you use your donation for the raffle ticket as an income tax deduction. Certainly this should not be the primary motivation for your raffle purchase, but it sure doesn't hurt. And if you win, consider donating a percentage of the win back to the cause.

Score a major inheritance? One of the factors you'll have to deal with (if you are even remotely sensitive) is survivors' guilt. How could you possibly enjoy the benefits of the extra money or goods if it comes at such a cost? You'll encounter a mix of reactions from friends and family. You might even hear the word "lucky" and want to cringe. Remember that the deceased wanted you to have this. That doesn't mean you can't donate a portion to a favorite charity, but it also doesn't mean you shouldn't enjoy this gift.

With both a game-of-chance win or an inheritance, think clearly about what you are going to do with the money. Consider putting it away for a while until you can think rationally. Is this the time to pay off the car or student loan and lift a debt concern? Better yet, can you change your life by cutting your credit card bills in half? And if you've already been good about managing your debt, maybe this is the time to splurge a little. Buy yourself the thing you always wished someone would give you as a gift. Or take the trip to see relatives or friends you haven't seen in a long while.

PAY DAY 1

Early in the game players hit their first pay day.

In real life, this can be either a celebratory or demoralizing time. In both the board game and in real life, you quickly realize that not everyone is making the same amount of money that you are. This leads to inevitable questions. Is the guy in the next office of more value to the world because his check is twice as much as yours? Should the fact that you make less than your boyfriend or girlfriend mean that he or she should pick up more of the tab for common expenses? Is a coworker who seems to do less work than you making more money? And what the heck is FICA and why does it need so much of your cash?

You'll be much healthier mentally if you don't treat your pay day as a barometer of your success. Lao-Tzu said, "When you are content to be simply yourself and don't compare or compete, everybody will respect you."

Just don't let that contentedness keep you from asking for a raise when the time comes.

Don't be surprised when you see how small your paycheck is. Between taxes, social security, and other deductions, your pay may end up bearing little resemblance to the offer you were made when you negotiated your salary. And until you buy a house, it's likely that your deductions will be minimal, so don't expect to get much back from the IRS.

But don't let that real-world number scare you away from sensible investments. Even though retirement is the furthest thing from your mind as you are embarking on your career, the power of the 401K and Individualized Retirement Accounts cannot be reinforced enough. Sure, it's much more fun to have $50 extra a paycheck for that new pair of cool-looking jeans or a few new CDs that you've been eyeing. But squirreling away money today to be used 30 to 40 years from now is actually very mature financial planning. When you factor in the employer match program that many companies offer (for example, you put away 3% of your salary pre-taxed and the company matches that amount for your retirement fund), it's much better in the long run to do without some extraneous material possessions now. Just remember to diversify.

ADOPT A PET

The impulse to adopt a pet is a good one. By adopting an animal you are giving a good home to a beast that otherwise, truth be told, may end up put to sleep because of the limited amount of shelter space available.

Choosing when to adopt a pet is almost as important as what kind of pet to adopt. Does it really make sense to adopt a large dog while you are still living in a one-bedroom apartment and working 18 hours a day? Are you getting a pet as a placeholder before having a child? Have you considered what's going to happen when your "I want a ferret" phase wears off? Still planning a summer in Europe? Consider putting off adopting until some of that wanderlust is gone or your pet-sitting fees might cost more than your trip.

When adopting a pet you have to think of the long haul. You have to assume that your animal of choice is going to be with you well into its old age. You have to factor into your life its needs, its medical upkeep, and its care.

It's a bigger decision than "a puppy/kitten is so cute." You have to commit to your newly attained live acquisition. Consider it a barometer of your emotional maturity level. If the thought of living with another being for the next 15 years scares the bejeezus out of you, than perhaps a long-term human monogamous relationship is still a long way off.

Perhaps you should start with a plant and see how that goes.

LOST!
LOSE NEXT TURN.

All of us stumble through life at least partly in the dark. On rare occasions, we find ourselves literally lost, not knowing where we are. As long as there is no apparent danger, this can be a mind-opening experience. You come to appreciate how much of the world—even how much of your immediate surroundings—you don't know. If you are in your car, you may become frustrated at the seemingly cavalier approach to signage that your destination spot has taken. You start to realize how many assumptions were made—and how many assumptions we make every day that someone will take care of us by showing us the way.

Being lost, though, promotes serendipity. If you aren't rushing to an appointment, the act of being lost can be a way to discover something new. If you've got the time, take the opportunity to stop into an unfamiliar store, to strike up a conversation with the person giving you directions, to learn about the places that you didn't intend to visit.

Approaching it this way, your situation becomes less a matter of finding your way out as it does maximizing what you do while there. Life is about the journey, not the destination.

Remember: X-rays and penicillin (and, admittedly, LSD) were all "discovered" by accident. And Columbus wasn't exactly looking to retire in Florida.

Of course, being lost can mean being unable to find your way emotionally or spiritually. The early post-college time can be a period of intense loneliness. More effort is required to see friends. Work can be disillusioning. Inertia can inflict your free time. Dr. Will Miller, in his terrific book *Refrigerator Rights*, talks about how depression is more likely to grow when we move away from family and friends (and thus have few people with refrigerator rights—people who are close enough that they can open your refrigerator without asking).

Lost and alone, it's easy to turn to the seemingly quick fix of drugs, alcohol, TV, and mind-numbing computer games. To fight such stagnation and to "get found," work to put yourself in the company of others that you respect. Find ways to connect. And don't be afraid to seek the help of a qualified therapist or member of the clergy. Although it may feel like it some of the time, you are not alone.

BIRTHDAY PARTY!

Used to be that every year, your birthday was more important to you than most national holidays. Now, though, you might be challenged to try to recall what you did on any of your last four birthdays. Sure, it's easy to ascribe significance to the 18th and 21st, but most of the others are more difficult to remember.

Why should a celebration of the day you arrived on this planet be more meaningful when you are seven than when you are 27? Shouldn't every year you stick around be more of a cause to celebrate, rejoice, and renew?

Perhaps it's a factor of the diminishing of the gift pile. You'll be lucky at 24, 27, or 30 to get a sweater from your parents or a dinner from your significant other. Perhaps it's the fact that there is too much else going on in everyone's life to take the time to celebrate your birthday. Perhaps you don't want to think about all the birthdays that have already passed. Perhaps you don't like to be the center of attention. But let's be honest: Everyone likes a little show of affection and support once in awhile. Doesn't everyone like to be lavished with the love of friends and family?

The solution: Strongly hint to friends that you'd like a surprise party.

Here's a guide to hinting:

Four months from birthday: "When I was little, I always thought it would be fun to have a surprise party."

Two months from birthday: "You know, there's a lot of people we haven't seen in a while. Maybe it's time to have a party at the house."

One month from birthday: "Maybe for my birthday, you and I should just go to dinner. An early dinner. I'd like to get home by 8."

If you've gotten no hint that something special is happening, then, two weeks from birthday, be blunt: "I'd really like to have a surprise party and I'll pretend to be really, really surprised so have one, okay. You don't have to tell me. Just have one."

ANOTHER BIRTHDAY POSSIBILITY:

Maybe you don't want to acknowledge your birthday. You may be one of those people
who don't want to be reminded that every time your birthday comes around you are a
year older. This is a futile position. You know from past experience that you can't hide
from this 1 out of 365 day happening (unless you are a February 29th "leap" baby, then
you might be able to hide from it three years out of four). If you don't choose to celebrate it, then use it for a day of renewal. To heck with New Year's—everyone is
resolution-spouting then. Take this day to decide the one thing you want to change
about yourself. And buy yourself a little something.

SKI ACCIDENT
Pay
$5000

Many of us have a drive to conquer mountains. Few of us have the nerve
or the resources to climb them. But convinced that it can't be that hard
if some of the bozos you know manage to pull it off, many of us take at
least one crack at hitting the slopes.

As you head up the ski lift, the blanket of whiteness is awe-inspiring.
As you take your position and look down the mountain, you start to
experience a bit of trepidation. But it's too late to turn around. (Of

course, it's not really too late to turn around. People have done it. But your ego is too invested in this.) So you push off, and you're on your way.

On your trip to the hospital, you stare into the face of the medic while you ask yourself what you were doing shooting down a mountain to begin with? What purpose did it serve?

These thoughts, of course, won't keep you from doing it again. We all accept risk in our lives. If we didn't, the passenger seats of cars would face the back, slicing a bagel with a knife would be illegal (bagel cuts are one of the leading causes of emergency-room visits), and condom sales would be booming. We take risks: some foolish, some life or death. It is part of our human make-up to take chances. That's what makes parents the nervous wrecks that they are.

The trick is to pick and choose which risks we take and to understand going in the best and worst possible outcomes.

WIN MARATHON!
Collect
$10,000

Winning a marathon is amazing. Participating in a marathon is equally amazing, at least to those who haven't even tried.

Those who watch may have trouble understanding the motivation of this sea of runners? After all, with the sheer number of participants, there is little chance of glory.

But what replaces the chance of fame is more important: The self-knowledge that you completed the task. You made it to the finish line under your own power. You went the distance.

"Do it for yourself," said nine-time New York Marathon winner Grete Waitz, "not on a bet or a dare or because 'everyone does.'"

As a solo activity with no equipment necessary, running is perhaps the most truly universal sport. The roads are always open, say the Nike ads, and they are right. "I always loved running," commented the great Jesse Owens. "It was something you could do by yourself, and under your own power. You could go in any direction, fast or slow, as you wanted, fighting the wind if you felt like it, seeking out new sights just on the strength of your feet and the courage of your lungs."

Of course, not everyone can run at the level of Owens or Waitz. More often, the runner may be that could-lose-a-few-pounds guy with the sweat-stained T-shirt gasping through your neighborhood. As you shake your head at his embarrassing form, just remember: He's out there doing it.

Apply this same thinking to other life goals. Know that, contrary to what you may have been told, some worthwhile goals will prove relatively easy to achieve. For instance you may be lucky enough to graduate into a lucrative job. However, other hard-to-reach goals may prove not worth the effort. You might sacrifice a significant amount of free time and damage an important relationship in order to impress your boss, only to find yourself caught in a round of lay-offs. In short, the world isn't fair. You aren't always rewarded in proportion to your effort. But that shouldn't ever keep you from trying what seems difficult or near impossible. Whatever the outcome, you will end up knowing a lot more about who you are—and who you've become—than you knew before.

SAY NO TO DRUGS/
VISIT A MUSEUM

THE GAME OF LIFE board game is targeted primarily to kids, so it's no surprise that this message is part of its do-gooder, revised edition (which has since been revised further to become Visit a Museum). No doubt you have already made your own choices in the matter. And as an adult, you are aware of the complexities of the issues. Wherever you've decided to settle on the matter, don't forget that you've got one life and only one body to live it in.

A visit to a museum is an inherently empathetic experience. Going to an art museum implies that you are open to the idea that other people see the world from a different perspective than you do. Going to a historical museum signals that you understand that people of the past saw the world through their own eyes—and that view is worth knowing about. Some stay away from such places because of preconceptions from school that are difficult to shake—the feeling that there will be a quiz and that material needs to be known in a memorized way.

Keeping museums in mind for your "what am I going to do this weekend" list is a way to keep yourself intellectually and spiritually engaged in humanity's ongoing struggle to figure out the world and its people. It's also a way to meet new, interesting people. Few museums these days have offerings limited to tours of their collections. There are often concerts, films, workshops, lectures, children's activities, and volunteer opportunities. You could pretty quickly become an expert on your town's history, in frontier life, or in the impressionist movement.

Keep your mind open.

CYCLE TO WORK/
DON'T DRINK AND DRIVE

It's very easy to fall into a routine when you've settled into working life. Monday's schedule is pretty much the same as Thursday's. There's no switching to a new class schedule every semester. You wake up, take care of bathroom business, grab a quick breakfast, hop in the car, and head to work.

Depending on your proximity to your office, though, you can vary your routine by varying your mode of transportation. Can you set out early and walk? What about riding a bike? If your office is too far away, apply the same idea to whatever short-hop trips are in your life. Is the library a mile away? What about the grocery store? Getting in the habit now of sneaking in a little exercise while also taking the time to appreciate what's between here and there can add significantly to your quality of life. It's a lot easier to nod a hello to a down-the-block neighbor from your bike. It's easier to strike up a conversation when you are on foot. By all means, use the car when you need to, but don't fall under its convenience spell at the expense of your bike and your feet.

Some earlier editions of THE GAME OF LIFE board game featured a "Don't drink and drive" space here. Is this different from the "Say No to Drugs" space? Consider that there are risks we are willing to take for our own lives and there are risks we take that involve those who are not part of the decision making process. Just as saving a life is something that becomes a never-to-be-shaken part of your being, so does taking a life. Ask a cop. Ask a war veteran. Ask someone who had a few too many drinks and plowed his car into a child.

Basically, there is never a reason to drink and drive. If you are so in need of a drink that you are willing to risk killing yourself or others, then you may very well have a drinking problem. At the very least, take the suggestion of comedian Todd Glass, who advised anyone above the legal alcohol limit to stumble to the nearest Domino's Pizza, order a pie for delivery, then hop a ride with the driver who is going to your house anyway.

With alcohol, the law conveniently tells you your limit. In other cases, there's no outside force dictating when you should end. There's no legal limit for a destructive relationship. You can't get busted for watching too much TV or spending too much time in Internet chat rooms. Understanding your own limits is something many people fail to do . . . at the expense of a rewarding life.

FLAT TIRE
LOSE NEXT TURN.

You spend hours in the car, having no real idea how it converts gas into movement. You just trust that it works. Now a simple thing—a nail, a small piece of metal on the road—has brought it to a stop. You curse. You thank the sky that the blowout didn't happen while you were doing 80 on the overpass. You try to get the jack to work.

And someone stops to help. You feel a little vulnerable, but you also feel good about the fact that people take time out of whatever they are doing to help. Not for money. Not for a favor. Just to help.

Of course how to change a flat tire is something that all drivers should know how to do. So why is it not part of the driver's license test? Make it a point to learn this skill. Then you can return the favor one day.

If the blowout has not yet happened to you, remember now what others have learned from experience. When you hear that tire go, your instincts may tell you to slam on the breaks. Don't listen to them. Instead, lift off from the gas and allow the car to slow down, moving steadily to the side of the road—even if the blowout is on the driver's side. The goal is to get the car stopped as far out of traffic as possible, with you safe inside.

That's the practical lesson of this space, but flat tires can also be seen as emblematic of the things that go wrong at seemingly random times. You need to go to an important meeting and your mother calls on the phone to talk about a family crisis. You're dressed for the date of your life and the clouds burst. The stomach flu hits just when your friends from back home are on the road to visit you for the first time in your new town.

Navigating unexpected obstacles is rarely fun. But as complications pile up, heed the words from a song in the musical *The Secret Garden*— "It's the storm not you/that has to go away."

You will get through this. It might not be fun, but you will get through it.

3

GET MARRIED

In THE GAME OF LIFE board game, marriage is mandatory, which probably has as much to do with societal standards as it does with the fact
that the game is just more interesting that way.

There are certain stages of your life when marriage—committing to
one person for life—seems as remote as the chance of flying to Mars.
And it should. Marriage is something you shouldn't seriously consider
until you've found someone whose presence in your life causes you to
seriously consider it. Marriage is not something you should do because
you have the major hots for someone. It's not something you should do
because it's the path of least resistance. It's not something you should
do because society says you should.

It's something you should do because you've found someone who
you can comfortably imagine facing life's toughest challenges with,

greeting the greatest joys with, and growing old with. Commitment is an overused word, but here's where it applies—when you've found the right person.

Most marriages don't last (the U.S. divorce rate is now closing in on 50%). But yours can, even if you come from a history of troubled relationships. How do you avoid the trap? Take responsibility. It is your job to overcome the obstacles. Decide unequivocally that your marriage is going to be a success. Then make it so.

How do you do that?

First, ignore the statistics. Make the commitment with the assumption that there is no exit strategy. You don't adopt a child with the thought that if it doesn't work out, you can return the child. Why treat marriage that way?

Second, understand that while you are going into this committed to the idea that this is the only marriage you are going to have, don't confuse the issue by assuming that this is the only significant relationship you are going to have. Your connection with your parents, your siblings and your friends are still of value. The details of those relationships will change, but their importance should not. Don't send the message that nothing else is important but your spouse. That's too much pressure for the both of you.

You are about to enter a world of major change. You probably spent your time from birth to eighteen in the primary care of someone else. You spent a few years sorting out your adulthood. Now you are accepting an emotional, physical, and fiscal partnership with another person. Big businesses spend years planning mergers. This merger is just as important—and can be just as complicated.

Bottom line: Consider the viewpoint of your partner. That means listening. That means empathizing. That means compromising. Decide which battles are worth fighting and make clear why you are fighting them. Don't focus on what you've given up for the sake of the marriage. Focus on what you've gained. In tough times, work to make this life better, rather than assume that there's a better life somewhere else.

AN UNSTATED MESSAGE:

One of the reasons we become jaded about marriage could be because of what we see on TV. The fact is, many times a wedding on a sitcom is an indicator that a show has run out of ideas: The walk up the aisle serves as a dividing line between when the show was good and when the show wasn't. Be honest, did these weddings really help their shows get any better?

Exhibit A: Rhoda

Exhibit B: Who's the Boss?

Exhibit C: The Nanny

Exhibit D: Mork and Mindy

Exhibit E: Caroline in the City

TV definitely seems to say that things get worse after marriage.

But that's TV. There are wide open spaces between the happily-ever-after of fairy tales and the downhill slide of desperate sitcoms. It's called reality, and what you bring to it will determine what you get out of it.

WEDDING RECEPTION
Pay
$10,000

This will most likely be the largest party you'll ever throw. And it's one that sends a message about what you value as a couple. If you are a guy, chances are you'll take the back seat in the planning. If you are a gal, odds are that you'll be battling parents, future in-laws, wedding planners, and well-meaning yet meddling friends.

It is a chance to both embrace tradition and blaze your own trail as a couple.

Some potential battlegrounds:

Invites: Everyone you ever knew vs. an intimate group: If you invite one second cousin, do you have to invite them all?

Music: Band vs. DJ: The music you actually like or the music likely to get people up and dancing?

Food: Buffet vs. sit-down

Seating: Head table vs. no head table

Goofy traditions: Garter/bouquet throw, etc. vs. not

Cake: Smashing into each other's faces vs. maintaining decorum

And, perhaps most importantly:

Attitude: Are you going to let your hair down and have a good time or are you going to try to control every detail (including whether or not your uncle sings) and make yourself miserable in the process?

For sure a wedding reception is a fun, exciting, joyous occasion. However, the real crux of your attention should be paid to what happens in the actual marriage. In terms of the money spent and the energy expended, one night pales in comparison to what is hopefully the rest of your life. Make this event the wonderful start to your life together, not the high point.

HAPPY HONEYMOON!

In days of yore, the honeymoon was a time to get to know your spouse. And not just in the physical sense. When marriages were arranged by elders or involved the stealing of a bride away from her family, the honeymoon was often the first real opportunity to see if you even liked your partner. One explanation of the origin of the honeymoon was that this was a hiding out period, marked by the cycles of the moon, while the bride's family either cooled off or moved along nomadically to other lands.

While these—and the traditional hanging out of the sheets on the morning after the wedding night—are largely relegated to the past, the celebratory aspects of the honeymoon aren't. While you are not able to run away to Cinderella's castle to live happily ever after, you can spend a day or a week or whatever your budget allows putting aside the rest of the world and spending some fantasy island time together.

In terms of destination, you and your new spouse need to decide what kind of honeymoon you want—relaxing, guided tour, low-key, or fast-pace. You could venture to the traditional places of American honeymooners of yesteryear including Niagara Falls and Atlantic City, or you can travel across continents. Wherever you end up, use the time wisely. Detox from the wedding (not just the drinking, but the build-up to the event that you now need to recoup from).

Fall in love again with your mate. Be reminded why you got married in the first place.

The trick, of course, is returning to reality afterwards: To understand how to translate the concentrated honeymoon time into workweek life.

INTERESTING NOTE:

In THE GAME OF LIFE board game, you—not the bride's parents—pay for the wedding reception. The honeymoon, however, costs nothing. Now wouldn't that be nice in real life?

BUY FURNITURE/ UPGRADE COMPUTER
Pay
$10,000

If you lived in a dorm at college, then the powers that be supplied you with the basic desk, twin bed, and couch. Your first apartment was probably put together from a combination of thrift shop, leftover-from-who-knows-who, and Aunt Tilly's 1958 sofa.

But now you —within your budget—get to choose what you're going to lounge on, where you are going to put your books, what are you going to eat off of, and where your stereo is going to sit. You're the one who has to weigh comfort versus style versus expense.

If you are living with someone, then your tastes have to be blended with another human being. What if you love contemporary styles and your mate is a country French addict? Perhaps the fact that you live with this person is a sign that you have at least similar likes, but do not fret too much if there are gaping discrepancies. There is a happy medium out there. In our catalogue-happy society, you can gaze at everything from Ethan Allen Furniture to IKEA in the comfort of your (albeit unfurnished) abode.

Start with the necessities. You need a bed. What size? If you like to spoon then a double may be sufficient. If you prefer to spread out and mark your territory then a larger bed is necessary. And, if you have pets that like to make their way into your nocturnal habitat, don't forget to account for them in your bed purchasing decision.

You also need a place to eat. Whether you have a breakfast nook or massive kitchen space, decide the importance of comfort in kitchen or dining room seating. If you plan on hanging around the kitchen table, leisurely drinking your coffee and doing the crossword puzzle, then cushiony seats are a must. If you plan on entertaining guests on a regular basis, factor them in.

Other items such as couches, chairs, stereos, and TVs should be purchased in order of need. If you plan on staying put for a while, it's probably a good idea in the long run to buy better quality stuff now so you don't have to replace it in a couple of years. And for crying out loud, remember to Scotchguard.

The most recent edition of THE GAME OF LIFE board changes this space to Upgrade Computer. The substitution is a little curious: What does it say about you if you are more interested in upgrading a home computer rather than buying furniture?

The question is: Why do you need an upgrade? In this computer age, it's easy to do such thing by rote. After all, every time you log on you are reminded that your Windows program was released in '95 or '98 or whenever. "Catch up," it seems to be saying. "You're falling behind."

But are you? Are you upgrading in order to better share photos and video with friends and family? Are you upgrading because the work you do at home truly requires the change? Or is it just that your computer's memory is packed with undeleted e-mails and games that you played once and forgot about? If it's up to the high-tech powers-that-be, you'll spend more time installing upgrades than you do actually using the computer.

The connection between furniture and a computer upgrade is to know what you need, what you can afford, and what the real benefits are likely to be.

CAR ACCIDENT
Pay
$10,000
if not insured.

All of us can remember the near misses. Some of us, unfortunately, can remember the direct hits. Even below the speed limit, it's a terrible feeling of force. We've all seen hundreds of car accidents on television and at the movies. Nothing prepares you for the real thing.

When it's not your fault, there's understandable anger. Beyond the pain, there's the annoyance of dealing with car insurance companies, rental vehicles, forms to fill out, etc. When the accident is your fault, those big-picture feelings can be even deeper. There are times when you are just not paying enough attention to the road. Or, someone being a pest in the back seat distracts you. Or you've come to believe that your cell phone isn't impairing your road skills.

Whatever the scenario, even if an accident is your fault, that doesn't mean it was intentional. However, you will have to live with that reality and the consequences of your actions. It's a burden few of us would want even our enemies to bear.

What can you do about it? At the risk of sounding like your mother, there are some ways to cut back on the dangers. Eat at rest stops, not behind the wheel. Pull over to make calls. Switch CDs at red lights. If you find yourself ignoring these easy rules, imagine that the other cars are filled with your family and friends.

SIDE NOTE:

This is the first time on THE GAME OF LIFE board where insurance comes into play. For many kids, this is their first exposure to the concept. The idea of insurance seems not quite right when you are a child. Why pay money if there's only a small chance of collecting? Why invest in failure? But in the adult world, insurance—automotive, health, travel, whatever—buys some relief from worry. It does what it says it is going to do: It insures you from financial disaster.

The question: **What is that worth to you?**

SPECIAL SECTION 1:

LIFE QUOTES

"Life is a banquet and all you poor suckers are starving to death."
–from *Auntie Mame*

"Life is just a bowl of cherries/Don't make it serious/
Life's too mysterious"
–lyricist Lew Brown

"Always look on the bright side of life."
-from Monty Python's *The Life of Brian*

"Life is what happens while we are making other plans."
–John Lennon

"I asked for all things that I might enjoy life. I was given
life that I might enjoy all things."
–anonymous Confederate soldier

"Life is a cabaret, old chum/Come to the cabaret."
–from the musical *Cabaret*

"We hold these truths to be self-evident, that all men are created equal, that they are endowed by their creator with certain inalienable rights. That among these are life, liberty and the pursuit of happiness."
–U.S. Declaration of Independence

"To life. To life. L'chaim."
—from *Fiddler on the Roof*

"Mama always said, 'Life is like a box of chocolates. You never know what you're gonna get.'"
—from *Forrest Gump*

". . . as one goes through life one learns that if you don't paddle your own canoe, you don't move."
—Katharine Hepburn

"A day for toil, an hour for sport, but for a friend is life too short."
—Ralph Waldo Emerson

"A different language is a different vision of life."
—Federico Fellini

"A man who trims himself to suit everybody will soon whittle himself away."
—Charles Schwab

"A ship should not ride on a single anchor, nor life on a single hope."
—Epictetus

"All you need in this life is ignorance and confidence, and then success is sure."
—Mark Twain

MOVE ACROSS THE COUNTRY/ ATTEND HIGH-TECH SEMINAR
Pay
$10,000

Sometimes growing requires relocation. You can dream about being a fashion model, but if you stay in Duluth, don't expect to do much runway walking. To assume that because you grew up in the mountains that you are a mountain person is to put too much trust in the fate of birth.

What do you lose when you move? Well, the proximity to family and established friends that have served as your support system can be a biggie. Then there's your entire ecosystem of your universe including, but not limited to, doctors, hair stylists, dry cleaners, and favorite local eateries. When relocating you risk losing your sense of self as you are presently perceived (which actually may be a good thing, read on...)

What do you gain? An opportunity to reinvent yourself. People have a tendency to think of others as they are upon first meeting. To your mother, you will always be, in some ways, the infant she first carried. If you start working with a company as an intern, you can take a few steps up the ladder, but it's likely that the boss will still see you as the green kid spending a few weeks away from college classes.

Also, a clean start is refreshing: New people. New places. New opportunities. Of course, this space on the board doesn't explain why you've moved across the country. If you are part of a federal witness relocation program, you're on your own.

If you play a more recent version of the game, you'll find this space instructing you to "Attend a high-tech seminar." This goes to some of the points discussed on the next space, "Night School."

NIGHT SCHOOL 1
Pay
$20,000

When are you done learning?

Some halt the educational process even before completing high school, taking healthy, youthful rebelliousness and turning it into a belief that valuing education means embracing conformity. You see it in many poorer inner-city neighborhoods—peer pressure to fail. Others assume the educational process is complete when a degree, whether from high school, college, or beyond, is earned.

Still others halt the process of formal education when they become pregnant or when a family's needs demand that they go to work rather than stay in school.

Whatever the case, it's helpful to remember that one of the greatest human traits is the capacity to change one's mind. Any literacy organization can share anecdotes about people who decided to learn to read at 30, 40, or 50. There are cancer patients with dire diagnoses who start learning to play piano after being delivered the bad news. Grandma Moses started painting well after many painters have retired.

If you already have a heavy load, know that anything added to it will make your life more complicated. No doubt you are working during the day or taking care of your children at home. Keeping your eyes open during class may be a challenge. Finding time for homework may mean giving up some pleasures. Try to find support among friends and co-workers. Brief your buddies about when to leave you alone—and that "no" means "no," even if there's a party going on next door. Consider a neighborhood kid as an in-house babysitter while you get some work done in another room. Check into your employer's continuing education plan. You not only might get encouragement, but you also might score financial aid or credit for time spent in class. Most employers want an educated workforce. They want to hire from within. And they want loyal employees to want to stay working for them, even when they have a degree in hand.

If a degree isn't important to you, and you are taking a course or two simply to further your knowledge on a subject, consider taking the pressure off by auditing a class rather than taking it for credit.

A life built on the idea that there's always more to learn is a life that rarely becomes dull. Even if you aren't taking formal courses, every book you borrow from the library or pick up from the bookstore is a course in a new subject. Go beyond the bestseller list. There won't be a test.

TAXES DUE

Up to a certain point in life, taxes don't seem to be a big deal. You've either had an under-the-table job where you didn't worry about paying taxes, or your employer took out a percentage of your pay that you never noticed, and that squared almost perfectly come tax time. You might even have gotten a little bit back.

Things change when you enter the land of grown-ups. With mortgage deductions, charity deductions, income from a primary job and a secondary one, expenses, investment income, 401K, etc., any reasonable person has no idea how much they owe the government (or are owed by the government) until all the forms are filled out. And even then, you never quite trust the calculations.

RULE OF THUMB:

If you've got more forms, papers, receipts, and statements than can fit comfortably into a manila envelope, hire an account or invest in tax-preparation software.

WIN LOTTERY!
Collect
$50,000

For the average American, the financial ladder can be climbed in a number of ways.

You could work for your fortune, of course, finding a career that will lead to increased financial rewards. But rarely does that lead to anything resembling millionaire status unless it also involves frugal living—something Americans are adverse to.

Increased financial status can come from savvy investing, or from getting in on the ground floor of a company with a generous profit sharing plan.

It can come from inheritance—waiting for that long lost wealthy relative to shuffle off this mortal coil.

It can come from "marrying up"—wedding someone of a higher status. And it can come from landing on the receiving end of an insurance settlement or lawsuit claim.

Or you can win the lottery.

To count on a lottery win is, of course, foolish. But people buy into it, taking the "Well, somebody has to win" stance as they drop their dollars on scratch-off tickets. We know that there are people who do walk out of a casino with a few more dollars than they went in with. And we know, deep down, that the odds are against us. But we don't realize how much they are against us. Faith in the lottery or casino gambling are symptoms of what author John Allen Paulos calls "Innumeracy." That is, our lack of understanding of math, basic or otherwise. We don't have a clear appreciation of the difference between a million and a billion. We don't grasp how how far the odds 1 in a 100 is from 1 in 10,000. While perhaps not as sociologically dangerous as illiteracy, innumeracy does affect our decision-making, encouraging us to take foolish risks.

So what happens if you win the lottery?

Much has been written about the percentage of taxes that get taken out of the big win, but no matter what the cut, you're still going to start out in the plus column. The question is, how long can you stay there? A sudden influx of money may mean a sudden influx of friends and family who never had time for you before. It can also mean you now need to be suspicious about people who now want to be your best friends and closest advisors.

If you are among the lucky group of lottery winners—and want to continue to lead a satisfying life—do an immediate assessment of the core of people who you can truly trust. This may only be two or three people, and that's okay. Have them advise you on every major monetary decision.

Sure, you'll now want to treat yourself to some things you always wanted, but square enough money away so that each year of your life will be easier than it would have been if you hadn't landed the win.

Consider quick gifts to those important to you. The longer you wait, the more people will wonder if they are going to get a piece of the pie.

Finally, don't be shy about seeking the help of your priest, rabbi, or other spiritual adviser. Most wealthy people either inherit the money or work up to it. Yours is coming suddenly. Don't blow it.

THAT'S NOT TO SAY THERE AREN'T GOOD USES FOR THE LOTTERY:

Take, for example, the man who used it to lose weight. To kick the candy-bar habit he had developed, he talked himself into buying a lottery ticket whenever he got a chocolate craving. Soon, he lost the drive for the daily Hershey bar. And he won $2!

VISIT IN-LAWS

It's said that you don't marry one person, you marry a family. To an extent, that's true. And there are plusses and minuses to that reality.

On the plus side, you've got a group of scapegoats—a crew to which you can act out your own feelings about your birth family without actually confronting your blood kin. Just watch how you are more likely to blast your in-laws when you are actually upset at your own parents. There's something about being an outsider in an inside situation that can liberate your tongue.

On the other hand, your in-laws are one more set of family members passing judgement on the way you run your life. Take a look at "Everyone Loves Raymond" or "All in the Family." These television shows are more realistic than you would like to believe.

But your in-laws don't have to be next door or across the street in order to meddle in your life in a profoundly deep manner. The slightest little disapproving glance over a new couch can send you reeling. Or, more impactfully, a comment on how you discipline your children can get way under your skin. The trick is to find a balance between keeping family harmony and maintaining a sense of independence. All the while, remember that life is short. Savor the moments and choose your battles wisely. And keep in mind that these people somehow managed to raise the person who you've fallen in love with. Maybe they aren't as dumb as you think they are.

BUY A HOUSE
DRAW DEED

If you think marriage is a commitment, wait until you sit opposite a realtor signing paper after paper after paper after paper...

There comes a point when you realize—or are talked into the idea— that as a renter, you are throwing away money each month. Apartment dwelling, you are informed, is only slightly different than renting a hotel room. You pay the rent, and in the morning (or at the end of the month), your money has been spent without investing in the future.

All true, but buy a house and your days of calling the landlord to complain about a leaky faucet or a noisy neighbor are over. You are now your own landlord and the plumbing problems are yours and yours alone. Just as you waited for the right time (and the right person) to marry, so, too, you should wait until the right time (and the right house) to become a homeowner.

WHEN IS THAT RIGHT TIME?

There are so many variables in that equation that it's impossible to come close to a single answer. For instance, it's possible you may never consider home ownership. Many very successful people go their whole lives without worrying about mortgages. If, however, you are grounded in a place with a low cost of living, you may consider buying a home even before you've considered marriage.

Some people wait until their family needs are so large that renting becomes difficult or impossible. It's not so easy to find a four-bedroom home with basement and attic for rent.

Some may opt to purchase when they realize that their friends are no longer going to help them move from apartment to apartment. And some when their rent payment gets higher than a good sized mortgage.

Whenever you decide to make the switch from renter to buyer, don't forget that this is most likely the biggest thing you'll ever buy in your life. Approach the decision wisely.

Consider: What can you afford? Your realtor will try to talk you into something bigger and more expensive than you may have thought you can handle. He or she may have a legit point: It can be very frustrating to find yourself outgrowing a home after only a year or two in residence. However, there is no guarantee that your income will continue to increase or that your job will hold out. Buying something today on the assumption that you'll be able to afford it tomorrow is rarely a good thing. Especially when you factor in such things as the cost of immediate and future repairs, and make a realistic assessment of what it's going to cost you to furnish the place.

Old or new? Do you like the feel of a place with a little history? Or are modern conveniences like closet space more important?

Cookie-cutter or personal design? Can you afford to have a house built from scratch? Do you have a need for uniqueness? Or is it good enough to go with a builder with a limited number of designs to choose from?

How important is neighborhood? Where you live means more than just what is within your walls. You need to be comfortable both inside and out. How important is proximity to work, recreation, and other locations (see the Cycle to Work space, page 45)? Is this an area where you'll feel comfortable walking at night? Do you love the idea of kids playing out in the street or do you hate the commotion? In today's world, neighborhoods are as in flux as the stock market. People move more often than ever, and a home purchase is no sign of permanence. If you are moving into a neighborhood because you know and like two of its residents, keep in mind that they could move in a year or two, leaving you behind. Similarly, a favorite restaurant can close.

However, on your visits to the home site, keep your eyes and ears open. If you hear dogs barking in the yard across the street, there's the chance that same pooch is going to be yapping when you move in.

There will likely come a point where you are burned out from the process. You'll long for the days when you slept under your parents' roof. You'll think that the perfect home is nowhere to be found. Don't lose hope. Just as in marriage, don't let anyone rush you into making a decision. So what if you have to rent for another month or two? If holding out for a year means landing a more permanent place where you'll be happy, don't rush in.

And once you've made the decision to buy, try to enjoy the process. If the house is being built from scratch, let yourself cruise into your new neighborhood to watch the beams being put into place. Appreciate the complexities of shelter and its implications. You are, literally, putting a roof over your family's head. Take pride in that. Imagine the pleasures that will be had in this new place. Soak up the notion that you will soon be home.

PAY DAY 2

Your first pay day as a married person is a significant one. Suddenly you aren't just looking at how the amount you are making is going to sustain yourself, but now you need to assess how this check is going to contribute to the upkeep of your family. And if you are like most couples and keep blended bank accounts, you have to adapt to the idea that you don't have total say in where this money goes. Your spouse could surprise you with a sudden household purchase, with an indulgence, or with a gift for you.

Fights happen over money—but the managing of money is one of the subjects often avoided or dismissed before marriage. Will you be jointly paying off each others' student loan debt? Will you have access to his trust fund? Will she have a say in where your 401K is invested? Do you need to reveal every purchase to each other? Who will be responsible for balancing the checkbook?

What if a great job opportunity comes along for one of you, but doesn't pay as well as you would like or need? One of you may decide that you want to go back to school. A terrific job opportunity could arise—in London. Discuss what sacrifices you are willing to make before he or she becomes your spouse. If you haven't had these talks yet, have them now.

START NEW CAREER

"YOU'RE FIRED!"/LOSE YOUR JOB

Being dismissed from a job can be a shocking blow, not only to your bank account, but also to your sense of self-worth and your commitment to a specific career. Whether the cause was your inappropriateness for the position, your inability to get along with a supervisor, or a downsizing due to company finances, it is difficult to get fired without feeling that you have somehow been lessened. You may feel as though you are not as strong as you were, as powerful as you were, as much a worthy person as you were.

Of course, the ideal is to recognize the red flags prior to the firing and be looking for a new position already. (Hint: When the boss asks everyone to write up a job description of what they do, layoffs are on the way.) You are much more marketable when you have a job and are looking, than if you are unemployed and desperate.

The pit is deep and the drop can happen quickly. If you've got strong family connections or rich friendships, then you'll have the sounding board to help pull yourself up. But it won't happen without your drive toward the future. And the future begins on the next day, the next hour. Expect to go through—not necessarily in order—the equivalent of Dr. Elizabeth Kubler-Ross' five stages of death: Anger, Denial, Bargaining, Depression, and Acceptance. After you've reached that final stage, the question arises: Are you in the right career? The trick is not to be gun shy because of what happened at one particular job or with one particular supervisor, but to seriously ask yourself if this is the kind of work you want to be doing in five years.

Even though you didn't elect to make the change, the time is now to do your assessments. Gauge realistically how much time you have until you must begin earning a regular paycheck. Find out what you need to do to maintain your health coverage (this is not a time to take the risk of getting sick, uninsured). Then look at all the possibilities. Don't announce too quickly what you are or aren't going to do. The old "close a door open a window" adage comes into play, and so does the idea of not burning bridges. Sure there are risks when you venture on a new journey, but life is not about the destination but the adventure along the way.

BABY BOY!

He arrives.

And suddenly you are completely responsible for another life—a life that screams and cries and drools and wakes up in the middle of the night and soils everything and changes moods on a dime. You'll get more frustrated than you've ever been in your life and you'll wonder how anyone else gets through this. Then he falls asleep on your shoulder and it all makes sense.

So what are you going to call this creature? There are hundreds of baby naming books out there. But what you name your kid isn't nearly as important as what you *don't* name your kid. If you want your kid's lunch money to ever arrive at school safely, avoid these: Orenthal James (and any other high-profile murder defendant), Adolf (and any other dictator), Carol (or any other name that usually goes to a girl), Trunculo (and just about any name out of Shakespeare), Cornelius (and any other name from *Hello, Dolly!*), Leif (or any other name that sounds great when you are high), Dick (or any other euphemism for a body part), Felix (or any other name of a cartoon cat).

Also avoid any name primarily associated with an ethnic group not your own. Irish-American couples should not, for instance, name a child Shlomo. Italian-American couples should skip Ling. Universality is a noble goal, but these just don't work.

Of course, a name is just a label and somewhat superficial. The act of becoming a parent is profound and life altering. Face the fact that there never really is a perfect time to have a baby. You could always have more money, a bigger abode, and a more stable job. But the life-is-a-gamble thing is true here. You are going to be more vulnerable and more emotional than you have ever been in your life. As a parent, you will feel joy, sadness, hurt, euphoria, and every other emotion under the sun deeper than you ever thought possible. You may move, switch careers, divorce—but you will always be parent to this child.

FURNISH BABY ROOM
Pay
$5,000

Pink for girl. Blue for boy. You can embrace the color/gender stereotype from square one, or take a different approach. Top-of-the-line crib? Antique rocking chair? Disney sheets or patterns without a licensed character? This is the stuff that your offspring is going to stare at for months. These things you surround your baby with will be his/her first sense of what the universe is all about. You want it to be friendly. You want it to be welcoming. You want the world to seem like a manageable place. You want a comfortable place for you to sit down with the baby. You want plenty of floor space for the baby to crawl around once the crawling begins.

The bottom line is that whether or not you go fancy schmancy or discount, the baby is going to spit up, poop, drool, and in general make a mess. Sure it makes sense to invest in stuff that will wear well if you plan on numerous children. But, choose realistically. You don't want furniture and accessories that might be ridiculous looking a year or two down the road. You want an environment that feels safe and exudes comfort.

BABY GIRL!

There she is, suddenly a citizen of the world. And you're responsible for at least half of what she is right now. Over the next days, weeks, months and years, the rest of the world will have its influence, but you will remain at the core.

You can't know what she will become. But you can know what sort of anchor you give her. You will, most certainly, evaluate your own life as she sleeps on your chest. You will ask yourself what you are proud of in your life and what you are not proud of. You will wonder what questions she will ask and how you will answer them. You'll see the link between mother and daughter stretching back to the beginning of humankind's presence on earth.

And just as history stretches behind her, it also stretches out ahead of her, into the future. Yes, you'll one day be waiting up for her to come back from a date, packing her up for college, perhaps watching her get married. All that potential is in her. The greatest gift you can give her is the opportunity to maximize that potential—and treasure her presence before the eye-blink that takes her on her own way.

WIN TALENT SHOW!
Collect
$10,000

Once out of school, most of us put our artistic talents on the back burner. Singers no longer sing. Guitar players find themselves practicing less and less. Painters are no longer celebrated with grades or student exhibitions. It's easy to forget that there is something apart from family, work, and the television set.

Why do we drop these passions? Part of it is an acknowledgment of reality. Every kid forced to take violin lessons is not going to be the next Itzhak Perlman. Every streetball player isn't going to find his way onto the L.A. Lakers. While you don't know who has that potential at 8-years-old, you have a pretty good idea by 18. Talent brings with it a huge risk of disappointment—of finding out that while you are good, you aren't great. And much of today's world demands greatness.

In the years before mass media, it was enough to be the best opera singer in the village. Today, local talent is compared to the national talents we see on TV and hear on the radio. It's much harder to be an audience-satisfying amateur today than it was a century ago.

Putting forth the effort to figure out if your talent is going to be your life's work comes with a price tag. There's a wonderful sequence in the movie *Searching for Bobby Fischer* when a New York dad realizes that his son has a gift; a genuine, almost scary talent for playing chess. He's conflicted over how to deal with that talent. Do you do everything you can to take the child as far as he can go with it? Or do you do whatever you can to keep the talent from getting in the way of the kid's normal life?

Remember: It's you who determines the goals of your endeavor, and whether you've reached them. Think you have the chops to win an international piano competition? Go for it. Satisfied tickling the ivories at family gatherings? Enjoy it. You don't need a stadium full of screaming fans to enjoy hitting a run-scoring triple during the ninth inning of a softball game. The best route is to find your bliss not in the rewards, but in the activity.

PAY DAY 3

Now that you have children, your pay may not seem to last long. And whether they say it or not, your childless friends—the ones who have given up on asking if you wanted to go out on Friday nights—are wondering why you didn't wait a little longer to create You: The Next Generation.

Things would be a little easier, of course, if you'd waited. But would they necessarily be better? Rationalize away. You wouldn't want your kids growing up in a rich home anyway. Where would they learn values if they had everything they want?

If money seems tight right now, look around you and see what can be trimmed from your expenses. Communicate with your spouse to make sure your lists overlap. Try to figure out *why* you are spending, not just what you are spending on. Isolate what is important. Much of American media is in the business of telling you not to be happy with what you have. New and improved is the order of the day. Last year's computer doesn't cut it. You've got to try the new restaurant. You're depriving your child if you don't rush out for the latest hot toy. How can you live without 300 television channels?

There is a very real possibility that you are making far more money right now—even adjusted for inflation—than your parents did at your age. Remind yourself of that. And hang in.

TWINS!

It doesn't really matter that the birth of twins cuts in half the time a woman needs to be pregnant to have two kids (duh!). It doesn't matter that you are encouraged for medical reasons to gain more weight than with a single pregnancy. It doesn't matter that the twins may develop opposite feeding and sleeping schedules (be sure to nip that one in the bud). Weighing the plusses and minuses of having twins vs. having two kids at separate times is a purely academic exercise, since it's an unplanned and random event.

What matters is that you've produced a pair. And the ordinary challenges of dividing attention between your new baby and your spouse and your own needs are multiplied. There are two diapers to change, two cries to contend with, two middle of the night wake-ups, two toddlers to follow, and two teenagers to teach to drive.

As in-vitro fertilization and other fertility treatments have been on the rise, expect to see more twins around (and, to a lesser extent, triplets and quads). Just look at any given pre-school and you are likely to see double many times over.

Avoid the urge to dress them alike. Avoid the urge to give them rhyming names. Avoid the urge to audition them for sitcoms. Take them out individually for special time. Remember: They are two kids, not halves of the same one.

BOX SEATS AT THE WORLD SERIES/
50-YARD-LINE SEATS AT THE BIG GAME

Pay
$20,000

The earlier version of THE GAME OF LIFE board game grants a pair of prime baseball tickets to the player who lands here. The later one changes it to football. Let's look at the diamond game first.

Unlike most other sports, baseball spends most of its time teetering on the brink of boredom. Ninety-nine percent of the time nothing at all is happening. Players run onto the field. Players run off the field. Pitcher stares at batter. Batter stares at pitcher. Umpire tells everyone whether the ball made it over the plate or not.

While watching a baseball game there's time to think. Time to let the mind race. Time to heckle. Time to debate the best baseball movies ever made (for the record, those are *Bang the Drum Slowly, Pride of the Yankees, A League of Their Own, Field of Dreams, The Rookie,* and an obscure silent comedy called *Speedy*).

One of the great things about a baseball game is that, until the final pitch, it is always winnable. If a football team is being beaten 35-0 and there's a minute left on the clock, you can safely leave the stadium. A NASCAR driver two laps back isn't going to catch up to a driver fifty yards from the finish line. But in the bottom of the ninth, a rally could bring a baseball team back from anywhere. It just takes hit after hit after hit. It ain't over, it's been said (and over said), 'til it's over. If nothing happens, there is at least the potential for something to happen.

Of course, during the World Series, you'll pretend that the game is a lot more exciting because there's a lot more at stake. This game is not going to end with winners casually shaking hands with losers. This one's going to climax with players throwing themselves onto each other in a pile of celebratory humanity. And decades from now, you will say you were there.

The same applies to football, although a fan rides a very different emotional roller coaster. In football, an interception or a fumble can turn the game around very quickly. Yet, there's a point of no return. With a minute remaining in the fourth quarter, few would hold out hope that a team down by 21 is going to pull things out. There's really no down time in a football game—no period of prolonged contemplation. As in a military battle, one side may exert just as much effort to gaining a few precious yards as it takes to score a decisive victory.

Which style best reflects your life?

ATTEND HOLLYWOOD MOVIE PREMIERE

Pay
$5,000

Americans love the movies. Not only do we, as a people, love the actual act of seeing movies on the big screen, we also love talking about them, spouting opinions on them, charting their box-office rises and falls, keeping track of what casts and crews do in their off time, and complaining about the trailers and reviewers who give away too many details. We know more about the making of movies than we do about the running of our government.

While you probably won't score tickets to an actual Hollywood premiere, it's within the realm of possibility that you could hobnob with stars and semi-stars at a film festival (take a look at *Variety,* the show biz newspaper, which lists dozens). More likely, you'll have to settle for winning a few radio-station-giveaway free passes to a sneak preview of a movie.

If you want to increase your chances of the latter, check out the websites of local radio and TV stations (you might want to register with a separate screen name to avoid getting lots of junk e-mail at your main address). The biggest plus is seeing films before the critics have chimed in or the TV chat shows have shown too many clips. As in life, we need some idea of what a movie has in store in order to motivate us to go, but knowing exactly what is going to happen takes the spark out of the experience.

HOUSE FLOODED!
Pay
$40,000
if not insured.

"A rising tide raises all boats." It can also raise you furniture, your insurance rates and your blood pressure when it comes in conjunction with heavy rains. Are the pleasures of living so close to the waters worth the risk of such potentially catastrophic events?

Being an adult involves making decisions about how much risk you want to assume for what potential upsides. That can manifest itself in your willingness to disagree with your boss, in your choice of recreational activity, or in your housing choice.

We don't always choose the safest place to live. Houses are built on earthquake fault lines, on the sides of mountains, in low-lying potential flooding areas. People buy in borderline neighborhoods that have a higher crime rate than the rest of the city. To the outsider, it may seem crazy to put yourself at such risk.

No matter how much risk you voluntarily assume, there is always a chance of trouble. So it's helpful to have your important papers and belongings in one place, ready to tuck under your arm in case of evacuation or quick move.

Here's a short list of what should be in the box:

Mortgage papers and deed

Insurance papers

Any bonds or other unrecorded notes of value

Birth certificates for your family

Your will

Letters of sentimental value

So much for the practical side. From a deeper perspective, an important aspect of an event—or even the threat of an event—such as this, is to assess what is really of value to you. It's clichè, sure, but it's also important to remember: the things you accumulate aren't what's important in life. Heck, in this game, everything of real value is right there in your little car.

BUY BIG SCREEN TV/
BUY HIGH-DEFINITION TV
Pay
$5,000

Whether you have an old school GAME OF LIFE board game or a new school one, this space is about taking the plunge into the purchase of the latest in TV technology.

It used to be that you bought a TV, plugged it in, and watched what was offered from a handful of network sources. You even had to get up from the couch and actually change the channel yourself! Now, most Americans have become accustomed to the idea of paying for television programming—whether by cable or satellite—while only a few Luddites and folks in unserved areas stick to broadcast.

But dozens of channels aren't enough. Along came home video and its souped-up brother, DVD. Now you don't just watch a movie, you watch the six documentaries, alternative takes, and outtake reel that go with it. Then you watch it again with the director's commentary.

And you have to watch it on a giant-screen TV. All the better if it's high-definition quality.

All of this adds up financially. To justify such an expenditure, it seems practical to spend more time in front of the tube (and surrounded by the requisite high-end sound system). And while the biggest problem may seem to be figuring out which remote actually turns on the TV and which controls the volume, the bigger problem is how much time this toy (and, face it, it is a toy) is eating up of your free time. No longer burdened with the excuse that "there's nothing good on," it's easy to park yourself in front of a great DVD and let your kids watch an extra hour of

Nickelodeon forgetting that there are other ways to be entertained. And other things to do in your spare time besides suckle on what critic Harlan Ellison called "the glass teat."

That doesn't mean you have to go cold turkey—just be aware of how much time you spend "amusing yourself to death" (to use the words of another critic, Neil Postman).

Go outside (you might actually meet your neighbors). Read a book. Do some volunteer work (two hours a week can really help a charitable organization). Visit a friend. Invite a friend over. Join a recreational sports league. And, yes, go ahead and play a game.

And when you do settle back to relax in front of the TV, really enjoy that time. Make real popcorn, not the microwave kind.

STOCK MARKET SOARS!

It happens. And you have nothing to do with it. But you've picked (or had someone else pick) the right stocks. Those companies did something right (at least in the short term), and so, on paper, you have more money today than you did yesterday.

It's a little scary, but it's also pretty cool to know that you own a small part of a company. You can go to stockholders meetings. You can make choices about the kinds of investments you want to make (local companies, environmentally friendly companies, tried-and-true companies). If you are contemplating a new job with a publicly traded company, take a serious look at what sort of stock options and other stock incentives are offered. With the right company, these can make a difference between a decent living and voluntary early retirement. Many a secretary has made it big by sticking with the right company.

Of course, if you don't do your homework and invest blindly, there isn't much difference between playing the stocks and playing the slots in Vegas. And that gambling aspect is accentuated thanks to the instant quotes and low trading costs available on-line. Day trading is addictive. Like playing in Vegas, though, you have to know your family's limits (and they have to know that you are playing). Have an advisor go over your buying and selling moves. If you find yourself playing just to play—or seriously believing that you've got a "system," unplug the computer and seek help from your local Gambler's Anonymous.

Now, with the market soaring, there's a strategic choice to be made. Because tomorrow you could have more. Or tomorrow you could lose it all. The world has gotten more complicated than just working for a set salary and subtracting your expenses from that. Thanks to your investment in the market, the potential exists—you realize—for you to become rich. And you are forever changed.

FAMILY PICNIC

The weekend is a relatively recent concept in human history. It signals a break from the day-to-day and echoes the Biblical story of God resting on the seventh day. George Saurat's famous painting *A Sunday Afternoon on the Island of La Grande Jete* and Stephen Sondheim's musical version of that painting *Sunday in the Park with George* both try to capture that sense of idyll: the notion of catching a moment of peace in an otherwise tumultuous world. A time to stop, briefly, to look out over the water. It seems so quaint. But it's also so necessary.

A picnic is less about the food you are eating and more about self-worth. Taking such a time out signals to yourself that you are worth the downtime. That work, and upkeep on your home, and all of life's distractions can be put aside, briefly, to take stock.

In many cities, picnics are associated with outdoor cultural events. Summer symphony seasons. Concerts in the park. Community film screenings. These are the only times we may take the opportunity to pack a picnic basket. But the parks are open daily. The summer may be shorter than we like, but it's longer than we give it credit for. There is time to do this. To heck with a balanced meal, pick some foods that feel like a treat. Splurge on an expensive piece of cheese and ignore store brands in favor of some frou-frou bread or crackers. Indulge in a decadent dessert. And do check the local laws on open container alcoholic beverages in public before bringing along that wine.

VISIT MOUNT RUSHMORE

There's something about western tourist attractions—The Grand Canyon, Monument Valley, Mount Rushmore, etc.—that sets them apart from their coastal brethren. Of course, there's the size. But there's also their sense of standing alone. These aren't destinations surrounded by other competing destinations. They are not places that run any risk of being dwarfed by anything, even the sky.

Each attraction brings with it a world of facts, figures, and anecdotes. For instance: Mount Rushmore, created between 1927 and 1941, consists of 60-foot busts of George Washington, Thomas Jefferson, Theodore Roosevelt, and Abraham Lincoln carved into the granite by artist Gutzon

Borglum and about 400 helpers. Not just a collection of popular prezes, the quartet represented the birth, growth, preservation, and development of the United States. (Those who propose adding another commander-in-chief should keep that in mind).

The first attempt to carve Jefferson's head proved a failure. The stone was not strong enough. The crew switched from Washington's right to his left and blasted away the old head. Big Mistake? Obviously such a mistake had no impact on the final awe-inspiring result.

No matter where you travel, resist the urge to be over-taught. Find a way to spend time away from the tour-guide's talk. These are places where contemplation should be the primary activity. Your job is to look around and get overwhelmed, to put yourself in context, to feel part of a unique place you may never be again. These places have the power to affect you in profound ways, if you open your eyes and heart.

CAR STOLEN
Pay
$15,000
if not insured

Most of us have returned to a crowded parking lot and forgotten where we've parked our car. We wander up and down the aisles trying to remember the surefire pneumonic device we were certain would help us keep track of A17 or D24. But now dinner has been digested and the movie discussed and that special letter/number combination isn't so easy to come by. So we wander and we imagine the worst.

Eventually, though, we stumble upon our set of wheels.

Usually.

When we don't, there's that moment of dread. The sense that someone selected your car from all the others to possess. Remember the last time you locked your keys in your car? How you cursed the difficulty you had breaking in? Now you wish it had been *more* difficult.

When you are victimized, what you need to realize is that there is a recovery time. Even if you are physically unharmed. Even if you were not anywhere near the scene of the crime. Don't dwell on it, but at the same time, don't underestimate the psychological injury. While insurance will likely cover the loss, putting you back behind the wheel in no time, the real item lost is your trust—the frustration from having first-hand evidence that at least some of your fellow citizens don't take the same basic moral stances that you do. Stealing is wrong. You just don't do it. When you buy something, it's supposed to be yours. It seems so simple. Unfortunately, it's not.

RIGHT FORK

FAMILY PHYSICALS
Pay
$5,000

"How long do you want to be around?"

It's a question that every doctor should ask a patient at every check-up. Because we don't just go to a doctor to be made well. We go to stay well. Or at least we should be thinking preventively.

If you are in good health, the annual check-up is an opportunity to reestablish contact with someone who should know at least something about you without looking at your chart. But your check-up is also a time for you to learn a little about your doc. Ask him or her about the family pictures, the autographed animation cell displayed on the walls, or if there's a vacation in the near future. Look at the diplomas. If the doc went to Georgetown, tell him about the time you spent in Washington. And don't underestimate the value of a good restaurant recommendation. Far from being opportunistic, these are simply steps to establish a connection. Remember: You can talk about your aches and pains without being a pain yourself.

As for your children's pediatrician, chances are ear infections, strep throat checks (gag!), and broken bones have led to more contact with him or her than with your grown-up doc. Hopefully you've chosen a doctor who won't make you feel rushed, no matter how busy his or her practice is, but it is helpful to come into a check-up with a list of questions and/or issues to be addressed. This way, if the doc begins to wrap things up sooner than you would like, you can whip out the list and recite.

TREE FALLS ON HOUSE

Pay
$15,000
if not insured

You've survived the flood (see page 81) but Mother Nature hasn't given up on inflicting damage to your home. Maybe it's revenge for ignoring all of those Arbor Days (tell the truth, do you even know what month it's in?). Maybe you thought you'd put off bringing in the tree surgeon even though you knew the oak was looking a little ill. Or maybe it was just a storm that struck your place at the wrong time. Whatever the circumstances, the damage is done and every glance from your shell-shocked family makes you feel like you should have known better.

Such looks can be among the low-points of parenthood. When you yourself are uncertain about your responsibility for something that has happened, it's hard to deal with the uncertainties of those you love. This is especially tough when there are branches in your master bedroom.

The important thing is that everyone is safe and it could have been worse. Children need to learn that everyone makes mistakes. And, that the next time a big old tree is looking sickly, you will react in a timelier manner. Look around: are there any potential disasters you're ignoring right now?

RETURN LOST WALLET

It's right there in your hands.

It's not like you deliberately took it from its rightful owner. It just appeared.

Finders keepers, right?

All of us want to believe that if we found a wallet on the street, we would return it to its rightful owner (surely there's an I.D. inside that says just who that person is). But what if there was $100 in it? Would that encourage you to pocket the cash and send the wallet? What if it was $1000? Does that change your actions at all?

Okay, Mother Theresa, what if the wallet belonged to a modern equivalent of Ebeneezer Scrooge? Wouldn't it be better to send the wallet back anonymously but give the money to a Cratchettish family?

THE REAL BIG PICTURE QUESTION:

Should our actions be based on what is right in the short term or what is best in the

long run? Is it better to hurt one person to ultimately save another? To give the question

an alternate universe spin, would it be morally acceptable to go back in time and kill

Adolf Hitler as a child? Okay, so we're getting way too sci-fi.

Where were we?

Okay, what if the found wallet contained $10,000—with no ID?

Or the ID of a convicted drug dealer?

Or the phone number of your favorite movie star?

RUN FOR MAYOR

Running for a public office is within the grasp of any American. Winning
may not be, but running is—just ask the transvestite from Indiana who
landed on the Democratic Congressional ticket even after calling the
press pretending to be former Charlie's Angel Tanya Roberts. (Seriously.)

What it takes to score enough votes for that office depends on the
size of the jurisdiction. Obviously it takes more to become the governor
of Texas than it does to become the mayor of Fruita, Colorado (which

you may know as the home of The Dinosaur Museum).

The decision to make a go at this or any other office carries with it assumptions that your grandparents didn't have to face: From small-town mayor up to president of the United States, your life is expected to be an open book. Opponents who want to ensure you are not elected will dig for dirt, whether any exists or not. The ability to topple a candidate is a fundamental one in this country, but one that effectively keeps many strong candidates from running. Say what you want about the last batch of U.S. Presidents, but how many of our families would hold up under the same microscopes that they found themselves under? We revere Thomas Jefferson and John F. Kennedy, but could they have made it into office under today's circumstances?

So what would it take for you to run for an office? Would it be a specific cause that you want to champion? Or would it be a general sense that you could do better than the last person to hold the office? Are you the kind of person who could make that decision on your own or would you need a group of people to convince you of your electability?

Finally, how would you gauge your success?

VOTE!

The Bush/Gore battle in Florida sent a clear wake-up call to non-voters from both sides (and from third parties): Not voting is a form of voting. By skipping a trip to the ballot box, you are voting for the status quo. By not voting, you help get into office the guy most popular with those who bother to vote. It may seem hip to be above all this political stuff, but you never are really above it. You are part of it. And the decisions made will affect you, even if you pretend they don't.

Clearly the presidential election is the one that gets the most attention—and the greatest voter turnout. But one could argue that local elections are where your voice can be heard even louder. The president of your school board may have much more of a direct impact on your life and the lives of your children than let's say, the Attorney General of your state.

Don't forget, though, to think before you vote. Being a rank-and-file party voter means turning over your judgment to others. And think about where your voting decisions come from. We want to pretend that the issues are what's important, but polls show that we respond emotionally to ads. The ratings go up when the issues are put aside in favor of the muck. We want to be better than that, but, as a people, we have yet to prove that we are.

Take advantage of election time to actually explore an issue—even if you only pick one. Read beyond the headlines. Laugh at the jokes and skits from late night television, but be aware if it is influencing your assessment of the candidates. And if you don't like what's happening, maybe it's time to run for office yourself (See the Run for Mayor space page 92).

TROPICAL VACATION/
BUY LUXURY CRUISE ONLINE

Pay
$25,000

Tropical destinations offer a few days of comfort, a few days of fantasy, a few days where recreation is available but not mandatory; where food is plentiful and has no calories (at least you can let yourself believe that). Here, the second toughest thing you have to do is ignore the unpleasant aftertaste of colonialism.

The first, if you are a workaholic like most people who can afford such a trip, is to keep cell-phone calls and e-mail checking to a minimum. $25,000 buys a lot of time away. Can your business function without you? And if it can, what does that say about your importance? Such thoughts can really ruin a parasailing excursion.

Don't let paranoia prevail. Prepare for your vacation not just financially, but also psychologically. Appreciate that downtime is not something to apologize for or feel guilty about. It's a necessary part of performing at your peak. To use a sports analogy, there's a reason why NFL teams only play one game a week.

NIGHT SCHOOL 2

Pay
$20,000

Nearly a third of THE GAME OF LIFE spaces have gone by since your last opportunity to go to night school. And here you are again, faced with the opportunity. It certainly will seem a little different now that you have more life experience behind you. (Although the same ideas of life-long learning being a key to ongoing happiness applies.)

This time, in addition to the educational benefits, consider the social ones. Night school is also a great way to replenish your friendship pool, especially if you've moved to a new city or just haven't found the kinds of friends you had in college and high school. Don't feel guilty about enjoying yourself. Yes, your spouse is home with the kids, but if you are playing on the same team, and you allow time for his or her separate pursuits, there shouldn't be any resentment. At least, not much.

Enjoy the dynamic of studying alongside students much younger than you are. Don't just look for similarities between you and your new classmates. Appreciate the differences.

LEARN CPR

A life stops. And it would remain stopped if not for you.

That same life restarts. And it's because of you.

Unless you are a police officer, fire fighter, member of the clergy, medical professional, or mobster, it's unlikely that life and death are part of your daily activities. The majority of us only face death through the people we know: The deaths of strangers are something confined to the obituary page.

But death happens all around us. Our ability not to think about that fact is one of the things that keeps us sane.

There is a chance, not a likely one, but a chance nonetheless, that you will be in a position to save a life. Having a little knowledge—the proper procedure for mouth-to-mouth resuscitation and chest compressions—can make a difference. To be blunt, if something happened to someone in your family, wouldn't you want a stranger there who has taken a certification course?

If you haven't been certified, go for it.

SPECIAL SECTION 2:
THE GAME OF LIFE
LIFE STORY

Milton Bradley, a lithographer best known for his beardless portrait of Abraham Lincoln, was 23 years old in 1860 when he created The Checkered Game of Life, a morally enriching journey that, in his words, "encourages children to lead exemplary lives." The game looks nothing like THE GAME OF LIFE board game that we know today (see for yourself: a board is in the collection of the New York Historical Society), but it laid the groundwork not only for the game, but for a toy empire.

In the first winter of sales, The Checkered Game of Life sold a very impressive 40,000 copies. But the game would have been just a Civil War footnote if it weren't for Rueben Klamer. In 1959, the head honchos at the Milton Bradley company hired the inventor to develop some product to help celebrate the company's 100th anniversary. Digging through the archives, he came upon Bradley's original game and, rather than duplicate it or update it, simply used it for inspiration.

The result was a game that took players from the start of an adult life through retirement. In the 1960s, it became even more popular when TV personality Art Linkletter "heartily endorsed" the game and lent his photo to the box. Linkletter's mug is gone now, but the game remains the same—except for some tinkering done in 1992, which incorporated "Life tiles" (bonuses along the way for do-gooder acts) and the elimination of such spaces as "Play the market." The company also added novelty versions, including a computerized version to its line. Here, when you get married, your spouse jumps out of the church, bounces on a trampoline and, after a few flips, lands next to you in your car. Pretty cool, although not terribly realistic (unless you've married a member of Cirque du Soleil).

ART AUCTION
Pay
$20,000

You can chart the evolution of a person by what he or she chooses to hang on their walls.

In most cases, it starts in teen or pre-teen years with taped or pinned posters and pictures. Eventually, those posters get framed and the pop singer and beer sign percentages graph toward zero.

At some point, original art may find its way into the equation.

Where do you start? Since most people aren't comfortable walking into art galleries to make purchase decisions, many of those initial original art purchases come from auctions. No, not the formal, paddle-wielding, surrounded-by-readers-of-*Art-&-Antiques*-magazine auctions, but the kind tacked on to charity dinners to raise a little extra money.

A few tips for anyone considering participation in an auction, formal or otherwise:

*Don't make your initial purchases as investments. Understanding the art market is like understanding the stock market—only your worthless stock certificates don't take up so much room in your garage.

*Art snobs may turn up their noses at your talk about whether a piece of art matches the decor of your living room. Ignore them. It's your living room.

*Appreciating a work of art is different than liking it. Perhaps a music analogy will help. John Cage is an admirable musician. But anyone who tells you he has Cage's music on frequent rotation in his disc player is a liar. Go with what you like.

*Go early to the auction and check out the goods. Have a dollar figure in mind for any of the pieces you are interested in. When that number is exceeded, walk out of the room.

HELP OUT AT SPECIAL OLYMPICS/ VOLUNTEER AT CHARITY EVENT

What is THE GAME OF LIFE board game about if not an ideal life? Despite some setbacks, every step points toward living fully while at the same time having respect and compassion for others. In the world of LIFE, you can have all the trappings of success while also being a person who lives by something like what the Jews call *"Tikun Olam"*—that is, an attempt to heal the world. Each of us has the power to make the world better, sometimes in big ways, sometimes in seemingly small ways.

Whichever version of the game you play, this space speaks to the fact that causes aren't just helped by those who have the wherewithal to sign big checks. They are also kept going by volunteers who do the grunt work. Whether it's a Leukemia Walk, a public television pledge break, a Girl Scout cookie sale, or the empowering Special Olympics, volunteers are needed to make sure that what is supposed to happen actually does happen. They are the ones copying and posting flyers, arranging for donations to be paid, helping with travel arrangements for participants, etc. If you aren't in a position to make financial donations to help out a cause, don't underestimate the value of your time.

WIN BEAUTIFUL BABY CONTEST/ WIN PHOTOGRAPHY CONTEST

Collect
$10,000

Vanity thy name is parenthood.

As much as you've given lip service to the "as long as it's healthy" view of offspring, there's still a shot of ego adrenaline that comes with someone telling you that you have a gorgeous child. Up that shot when the judgment comes from a body sanctioned to hand out ribbons.

Of course, the fact that you entered the contest to begin with says something. You can rationalize that you are helping to support a local event, that it is all in good fun, that it's just the opinion of a few judges and what does it really matter. But confess: You have checked out the competition and noted every case of infant acne and lumpy-headedness. You've separated out the criers and the heavy droolers and the just-plain ugly. (Yes, some babies are ugly. Don't pretend you didn't notice.)

There is a lot of debate about beauty pageants as children, particularly girls, get older. Who is the pageant really for—the parents or the child? How does the little girl feel if she is not picked? What kind of message are we sending children when we slap make-up on them and put them in frilly clothes? Yes, life is full of competition. And, life is not always fair in terms of who wins and who loses. But do children need to experience needless disappointment at such a young age?

The latest edition of the game switches this to a photography contest. The assumption is that you've snapped something yourself that has earned an award. That could mean that you were at the right place at the right time and caught a particularly dramatic or funny image. Or it could mean that you carefully composed a shot that is worth the proverbial thousand words. Of course, it could also mean that everyone else who entered the contest didn't know an aperture from an appendix.

The amount of the prize, though, indicates that this was something serious. When your hobby earns such acclaim, it's time to consider: Should you rethink the way you are spending your time? Many a photographer, writer, and composer has peaked later in life. Reconsidering your career may just be a sign of the times, it could be a mid-life crisis, or it could be that it's time to seriously consider exploring new territory.

While we're on the subject of photos, award-winning or not, here's a bit of advice: Try to put your "keepers" in photo albums as soon as you can. Pictures can get backlogged to an absurd degree, rendering them almost meaningless. The sooner they are organized, the more likely they will be a source of enjoyment rather than a boxed burden.

LEFT FORK

TAXES DUE

Again...

And again...

And again...

TENNIS CAMP
Pay
$25,000

You don't see many people over 40 playing football. You see few out on the baseball diamond, and even fewer playing street hockey. But only golf (and maybe bowling) rival the popularity of tennis among the 40-and-older set. And tennis certainly provides a better workout.

Of course, you have to enjoy face-to-face athletics—as opposed to the side-by-sides of running, or the scattered teams of baseball. Tennis is closer to fencing or chess than it is to most other sports. Once you master the basics, it's an ongoing attempt to out-strategize your opponent.

Picking up this or any sport when you're older (look, you're more than half-way through the LIFE board) is different than doing the same as a child or teenager. There's no illusion here that you will one day become a superstar—or that you could if you just focus hard enough on your backhand. Instead, you can get a little more philosophical about the game. Isn't this fancified version of "keeping the ball in the air" really about being able to return whatever life throws at you?

AFRICAN SAFARI/
DONATE COMPUTER NETWORK
Pay

Old school and new school GAME OF LIFE boards differ dramatically on this space. In the one case, you are journeying to a fascinating continent.

In the other, you are involved in some high-tech charity work.

First things first. The notion of an African safari has changed since Hemingway's day. Where once it called up images of macho men in pith helmets armed to the teeth with enough firepower to knock out a pride of lion, it now is more likely to feature photographers whose only shots are the ones captured on film. Travel agencies are built upon such high-end travel, all trying to minimize the hidden dangers of safaris (i.e. virus-spreading mosquitoes, wild-animal attacks).

But why do we want to go? The animals are closer at the zoo. The accommodations are rugged to say the least. The heat, well, there's a reason for the expression "Africa hot." But that discomfort is part of the draw. This is reality. You know from Animal Planet documentaries and Jane Goodall books that there are places where human beings are in the minority. But, in your gut, you never quite believe it. Everything in the civilized world sends the message that mankind is in control.

A safari—or, to a lesser extent, a hike deep in the woods—takes away that illusion. It's possible to create a device that transports human beings to the moon. It's possible to release the power of impossibly small atoms. But it's impossible for any group of human beings to create a veldt, to build a mountain, to generate an ocean. In the silence of the fields, the preciousness of the planet can be heard very clearly.

Now, about that computer network: Bully for you. Obviously you've become a success in life. Understanding that other people may have use for your discards can make the difference between a school being on-line and a school being out–of–touch. Or you may help a not-for-profit organization run more effectively. Your donations don't have to be on the scale mentioned here, though. Take a serious look at what you are throwing away. Is any of it of possible use to anyone?

STOCK MARKET CRASH 1

And so it goes.

You were a genius there for a while. You watched the value of your portfolio rise and you felt somehow above all the risk. You could have cashed out on Monday if you felt like it, but then Tuesday loomed and since that line on your portfolio web page had been moving up faster than it had been moving sideways, well, why bail now? Only a fool would sell now. Tuesday looked good, too, and while the rise wasn't as steep, it still ended with more for you on paper than it had since, well, forever. Money for nothing. No effort. No pain. Tomorrow you'll cash out, you say to yourself, and start figuring what you'll do with your sudden gains. A new car? Pay off some credit cards and finally be out of debt? Down payment on the new house?

Wednesday morning shows a slight dip, which surely will correct itself by the closing bell. You obsessively check your portfolio online, watching what you thought you had slip down to lower levels than it was on Monday. But it will come back. Has to. And you repeat the same thing Thursday when your portfolio seems to be in free fall. You want to bail, to get out with what you put it, but you have seen how high the peak can go. What fool would bail at this point? There's a track record now, and if it was up that high once, why can't it be there again?

And so you wait.

BE MY VALENTINE

In a nutshell, Valentine was a priest in Rome who helped out some folks being persecuted by Claudius II. The emperor did his best to get him to renounce his faith; he held up and, for his troubles, was beaten with clubs and beheaded. Now pass the chocolate hearts.

The meaning of a valentine differs dramatically depending on the ages of the sender and recipient. Grade school students are encouraged to bring Valentine Cards for the whole class. This keeps feelings from being hurt, and it also keeps any meaning from being attached. When "I love you" is followed by "I love everybody," it may speak to a Universalist way of thinking, but it doesn't carry much in the way of romance. A radical solution: Just as adults shouldn't go trick-or-treating, children shouldn't bother with Valentine's Day. Sure, it would be tough to end the tradition, but not if the actual story of St. Valentine were stressed.

In high school, Valentine's Day can become a way of letting a member of the opposite sex know that you are interested. A sent flower. A passed note. It may be hip to mock Hallmark cards, but that doesn't mean that you don't still get a charge out of knowing that someone, somewhere, is interested in you.

For many guys from teens on up, Valentine's Day is a day to dread, fearing that you won't live up to whatever expectations your significant other may have for you. Can you possibly be romantic enough, buy the right gift, pick out the right card? For established couples, Valentine's Day can be a base-touching time. An excuse to express your feelings.

For women who don't feel liberated enough to take the initiative, the day can be one of waiting and wondering. For those gutsy enough to make the first move, it's an excuse to send some flowers or a card and make one's interest known.

However, if you'll excuse the cynicism, it's hard to ignore the fact that the same candy that was $48 on Valentine's Day will be $24 on February 15th. A dozen roses, which usually cost $40, can go for $100 on V-day. You can be just as romantic the day after without breaking the bank. Heed this advice: on the day after Valentine's Day go to your local store with your sweetheart and raid the 50% off candy aisle. It's fun, silly, and you get more bang for your buck. Sneak the candy into a movie. Love each other.

OBSERVATIONAL NOTE:

There are no divorces or separations in THE GAME OF LIFE board game.
Could be because from the moment of marriage, that spousal
peg is always in the car right next to you.

DAY CARE

Pay
$5,000
per child

You've birthed a child. You've also birthed a career and have bills to pay. For many, the decision about who should take care of your child is a painful one.

Although it may be too late, the first step in the daycare dilemma should be to talk with your partner before you even consider having a child. The first question: If we have a child, do we both still *need* to keep our jobs? The second question: If we have a child, do we both *want* to keep our jobs? Carefully do the math. You may be surprised to figure out that after taxes and childcare, a second income may not be as fruitful as you thought.

If you both need to keep your jobs for financial reasons, then choosing an appropriate day care setting is critical. You first must decide what type of setting you feel most comfortable with. Do you prefer a day care center or a home environment? Do you want—and can you afford—someone to come to your house? Would you consider an *au pair* in your home?

There are a multitude of things to do next. You need to carefully check references. Talk to people who have had their children under the care of your chosen provider. You also need to check the policies on caring for sick children. Is there any flexibility in drop-off and pick-up time? You are entrusting your child to someone else's care for approximately 9 hours every workday—not that you want to think about it, but this is more waking time than the child will spend with you.

And remember: This is a human being, albeit a small one, that you are dealing with. Let your child spend some time with the child care person prior to starting a full-time gig. And prepare for the tears, both yours and your child's, that will come as you walk down the steps alone.

Parenthood is not easy, and this is one of the toughest parts. Keep your eyes on the prize: Having a happy, healthy family. Make your decisions accordingly.

WRITE BEST-SELLER
Collect
$80,000

Penning a best-selling book doesn't necessarily mean creating a work of lasting literary merit. The bestseller lists are filled with volumes of cartoons, self-help tomes, celebrity bios, and novelty books. And while poets and serious fiction writers may scoff at such undeserving works, the reality remains that any book on the list—with some help, perhaps, from savvy marketing—has caught the attention of the masses.

To bring pleasure, diversion, or instruction to hundreds of thousands of people is no small thing. It's a peak that someone on a standard career path—someone thrilled with a $500 holiday bonus—can't know. It's also a potentially numbing challenge: Will they like me this much next time? And what will it mean if they don't?

While the rewards are many, it's important to remember that your self-worth cannot be tied to the fickle taste of the public. And no matter how successful the book, it won't be long before it appears on the $5-or-less discount pile. Or drops from the radar altogether. How many readers can recall such once-top-of-the-chart books as 1910's fiction bestseller *The Rosary* by Florence Barclay or the 1966 blockbuster pop poetry collection *Stanyan Street & Other Sorrows* by Rod McKuen? Even more recent bestsellers can be easily forgotten by a public with a short attention span. To keep yourself humble, remember that a movie that totally bombs is seen by more people than read an average best-selling book. But don't let that stop you from going for it.

Remember that no book ever made the best-seller list without being written. As Hugh Prather said in his book *Notes to Myself*, "If the desire to be a writer is not accompanied by actual writing, then the desire is not to be a writer." Set out first to write the best book you can, regardless of the genre. If fame and fortune come, that's dessert after an already satisfying meal.

ADOPT TWINS

Adopting indicates parenting free of ego. It's a sign of understanding that parenthood is not synonymous with seed-supplier or egg-supplier.

For some, the instigation to adopt begins with an inability to have children biologically. For others, it comes from a desire to help those youngsters who have been given a raw deal for one reason or another.

Adoption brings with it unique challenges. One of the unpleasant—and underreported—facts in the adoption world is the number of cases where an adopted child is returned by the adoptive parents. This often happens in special-needs adoptions—situations where kids from troubled or abusive backgrounds are placed in adoptive homes. Well-intending parents may not fully understand the challenges they will be facing. While family therapy (both prior to and during the adoption process) may go a long way to help such situations, adoption is not a single event; rather it is a life-long process. In the last few years, adoption advocates have worked to bring this bipartisan topic to the forefront of this country's attention. The average person today is less likely than in the past to differentiate between adopted children and "real" ones. And adopted kids are taught how blessed they are not only to have people who brought them into the world, but also parents who accepted the hand off and gave them their love.

The fact that such an unusual space is included on THE GAME OF LIFE board is curious. The fact that there are parents out there who will adopt twins, keeping such bonded siblings together in one family, is remarkable.

INVEST IN BROADWAY PLAY
Pay
$15,000

There are few more foolhardy investments than a Broadway play.

First, it's helpful to distinguish between a play and a musical. In entertainment industry parlance, a play is a non-musical production—and it would be a safe bet to guess that the average person couldn't name a single play that has been performed on Broadway in the past five years. Where once thrillers were a staple, kitchen-sink dramas ruled, Neil Simon offered a streak of a-new-one-every-year comedies, and such great American playwrights as Eugene O'Neil and Arthur Miller were kings, now the New York theater district is made up of musicals and little else.

But even those aren't smart investments. At least if you put your money in a movie project, there's the chance of video, foreign, and cable sales if it doesn't make it at the Cineplex. On Broadway, a show in development for years can close after opening night if the critics are harsh and the box-office phones aren't ringing.

Still, you can invest in theater without doing much gambling. There is at least one not-for-profit theater company in most major cities. These groups—The Hartford Stage, The Goodman Theatre, The Actors Theatre of Louisville, The Oregon Shakespeare Festival—do world-class work and bring theater to audiences beyond the high-ticket-price Broadway houses. To invest in them is not only to invest in great theater, but also to invest in the cultural life of a region. The $15,000 you give up on this GAME OF LIFE space would go a long way toward helping a theater company repair its seats, stock its costume department, upgrade its lobby, or spread the word about its work. It can also affect the work itself, allowing a company to bring to town a playwright, director, or cast member. And you get to sit there—in the front row if you like—knowing that, even without a theatrical talent, you were one of the "angels" who made it possible.

JOIN HEALTH CLUB

After college, it's not as easy to stop into the gym to shoot some hoops, lift weights, or play a game of racquetball. The demands of work and family significantly narrow the time required for working out.

Health clubs know this. They know that you feel guilty about it. They know that you fear your body slipping away from your control. And they want to sell you on membership often with less scruples than the stereotypical used car salesman.

As you consider joining a health club, keep in mind these tips:

*Go for convenience. You'll get far more use from a modest facility near your work or home (or somewhere on the route) than you will from a state-of-the-art gym that's not on your beaten path.

*Find a place where you'll be comfortable. Does being around the opposite sex motivate you or intimidate you? Would you rather be in a place where everyone is more buff than you or where he or she is facing the same challenges? Do you like TVs on while you navigate the tread-mill or not?

*Check out the potential gym during the times and on the days when you are likely to use it. Saturday afternoon could be a very different scene than Tuesday evening.

*Commit yourself to a schedule. If your gym time is flexible, you probably won't be doing much flexing.

*Take advantage of offers early on to develop a workout strategy—or make a few personal-training sessions a condition of membership.

*Above all, remember the reason you are there: a healthier life is a more satisfying life. It's easier to meet life's challenges and take advantage of its opportunities when you aren't winded from the journey.

FAMILY PORTRAIT

Pay
$35,000

Whether snapped at the local discount store or by a budget-breaking pro photographer, whether painted by your cousin or by a gallery-showing artist, a family portrait is the freezing of a moment in time. In an increasingly informal world, it's an opportunity for your clan to dress up and become your idealized selves—at least for the length of a flash.

It may all seem so temporary and a bit silly. But it only takes a few months for you to realize how much bigger the kids are already or how much more gray hair you have. Use this as an opportunity to take stock of who you are and what you have.

Tips for a good portrait (photo):

*Wear clothes that are understated and preferably monochromatic. But don't wear attire that will make you look washed out.

*Everyone should wear something that is at least coordinated with what everyone else is wearing. No, that doesn't have to mean matching shirts, but at least outfits that blend well.

*Think long and hard about your hair. Do you want your descendants to know you with an up-do that would frighten the Frankenstein monster?

*Try not to be angry with each other. Even if it doesn't show in the picture, every time you look at it you'll remember why you were pissed.

Tips for a good portrait (painting):

*Make sure the artist is clear about how realistic vs. how idealistic you want this to be. In other words, do you want a little nip-and-tuck work on the neck or not?

*Future generations will read into how you are positioned in proximity to each other. Be aware of context.

*Don't biggie-size the picture unless you have a biggie-size place to put it. Be conscious of where you plan to hang this thing.

Tips for a good portrait (sculpture):

You're kidding, right? Get over yourself.

BUY SPORTS CAR/
BUY SPORT UTILITY VEHICLE
Pay
$25,000

It's only a small word difference, but there's a big difference between the mid-life purchase of a sports car (old school GAME OF LIFE) and buying a sports utility vehicle.

Buying the sports utility vehicle indicates a desire to ride the rough terrain. While most SUV buyers won't go anywhere near the creek beds and sand dunes indicated in the car commercials, the knowledge that you could cruise these locales if you wanted to has a great deal of psychological value.

Still, there are few purchases as fun as cruising the streets with the top down on a brand-spanking-new red convertible with the right music playing on the radio ("Boys of Summer" anyone? "California Girls"? "Twistin' by the Pool"?). Sure, it's frivolous, but as long as you don't take it too seriously, why not enjoy it?

Just remember that it's you in the car. Not Suzanne Somers enigmatically smiling in *American Graffiti*. Not Ken on his way to the Barbie dream home. A 45-year-old guy in a great car is still a 45-year-old guy. Buy it and drive it and feel good in it because you enjoy it, not because you think it's going to bring back your youth. Say goodbye (and good riddance) to those days. Embrace whatever age you are and make the most of it.

Just wear your seatbelt. And keep in mind that the cops can see you with the top down.

TAX REFUND!
Collect
$75,000

If your best friend said, "Here, I've been holding your money all year and now I'm going to give it back to you," you wouldn't feel like he's given you a gift. But that's how we react to a tax refund. Still, this is one case where we've universally decided that it's better to receive than to give.

Want to help improve your chances of a refund? Here's the four tips that experts say are the most common mistakes made on income tax returns:

1. Missing, illegible, or incorrect social security numbers.

2. Simple math errors. Like your grade-school teacher said: Double check your work.

3. Reading the wrong income line from the tax table. If you need to, use a ruler.

4. Write "United States Treasury" on your check, not "Internal Revenue Service." It's not a big deal, but it's the government's way of letting you know that your hard-earned money is going toward running the country, not simply paying for your audit.

RIGHT FORK

HOST POLICE CHARITY BALL
Pay
$15,000

Giving to the policeman's ball used to be another way of saying "bribery." A few dollars to the fund might get a speeder out of a speeding ticket or get an officer to look the other way over an expired license plate. At least, that's what old TV and radio shows seemed to be implying. A minor problem? Perhaps.

Yet even with 3.1% of the U.S. population incarcerated, we still have the feeling that cops aren't doing everything they can to catch the bad guys. Some take that fear and use it to rationalize any behavior on the part of cops. What's a little brutality if it gets the punks locked up? Others see the prison population figure as a sign that the system we have isn't working. And while most cops are sending a peaceful message, it just takes a few to change the public perception that that's the goal.

As grade-schoolers we were taught that the police officer is our friend, but on the street, we saw teens trying to avoid encounters with cops. We were told to go to a guy in uniform if we were in trouble, but then we overheard our parents expressing dread at the sight of an officer when they were going a tad over the speed limit. Even now, we're not sure how to feel as television news reports both police brutality caught-on-tape and flag-draped funerals of officers who gave their lives to protect us. Like soldiers signing up for a lifetime of duty, someone beginning training as an officer knows that his or her life will be on the line.

We admire that. And it seems to scare us. It reminds us that even in the greatest country in the world, we need to be protected.

FIND BURIED TREASURE!
Collect
$80,000

THE GAME OF LIFE board is filled with financial windfalls. And this is one of its silliest.

But let's broaden the metaphor a little. A buried treasure need not be something left by pirates. It could be an unexpected find at a garage sale. A Tiffany lamp sitting in your grandparent's attic until you discover it. A rare postage stamp passed down from a collecting relative.

It need not even be something with monetary value. It could be a forgotten letter—one from yourself that reminds you of the person you've evolved from. Or a memory box of your child, telling you to hold fast to the moment you are in, because it goes by so quickly. It could be memorabilia collected by your parents or your grandparents, asserting from the past that their days and weeks were just as long and as full of life as yours.

Such treasures should remind us that things, even important things, can slip from our lives. And that equally important things, things we've long forgotten about, can be found.

DONATE TO ART INSTITUTE
Pay
$25,000

In a world with poverty, hunger, and disease, it is sometimes difficult to rationalize donating money to something as seemingly non-essential as an art organization. With the names of wealthy donors already crowding the displays, art carries with it the burden of perceived elitism. What could some oil on a canvas possibly do to help the masses?

A lot, if you ask writer Leo Tolstoy. In a letter to H.G. Wells, he said, "Art is a human activity consisting in this, that one man consciously by means of certain external signs, hands on to others feelings he has lived through, and that others are infected by these feelings and also experiences them."

Art reminds us that there is something to strive for besides simply survival. It reminds us that there is not just one way to look at things. It allows us to see the world through another's eyes. It says that it is possible to create something that can last for generations or even centuries.

In the end, by establishing that the artist's unique viewpoint is worth preserving and paying attention to, it implies that each person's viewpoint can be valuable.

RECYCLE

Used to be that driving your trash to the recycling center was worse for the environment than throwing the stuff away. But with the increased availability of curbside recycling service (and, if not that, then recycling bins appearing in shopping mall parking lots and other easy access areas), there's little excuse not to recycle in areas where it's available.

Of course, recycling is only the third step in the environmental "R" triad. The first two are Reduce and Reuse. Use less when possible, or use goods that come in less wasteful packaging. Find secondary uses for the things you do use. Then recycle.

To be honest, it's all a pain in the butt. But nobody said that doing your part to leave the world better than you found it was going to be easy.

TV GAME SHOW WINNER!
Collect
$95,000

Another financial windfall from THE GAME OF LIFE folks, this one satisfying the fantasy we have of being rewarded for our knowledge, our skill, our strategy, or our dumb luck.

From our comfortable seat at home, it's easy to feel superior to the guests on television game shows. We cringe at their inability to articulate in the brief "get-to-know-you" segments that lead off most programs. We yell at the screen when we know an answer before they do. We ignore the questions we don't know and concentrate on the ones we do, convinced that this proves that we, not they, deserve a share of the winnings.

What we tend not to do is recall the difficulty of answering questions under pressure. We forget that the player is faced with lights, camera, action, a studio audience, and the knowledge that millions at home will witness the competition. We forget the time we were at a party and couldn't remember the name of the host. The blanking-out moments when time was running out to fill an academic blue book. The time spent roaming the bookstore trying to remember the name of the novel that was recommended just the night before.

If we paid attention, game shows would remind us that we are not computers. We don't know everything and we don't have instant access to everything we do know.

NOTE TO GENETIC SCIENTISTS:

One thing the world could use—should you find yourself with some research time and excessive grant money—is a line-item veto for your brain. Wouldn't it be great if you could have a list of all you know…and the ability to eliminate the stuff that's taking up space? Trivialities, unwanted, fly into our heads while the important facts, the ones we need—lose a fight to rise to the surface. A little brain purging could do the trick, wiping out all those commercial jingles, old gym-locker combinations, and '70s lyrics. Sure, they might help when we make it onto *Jeopardy!*, but how many of us are going to do that?

SUMMER SCHOOL
Pay
$5,000
per child

When a child attends summer school, that's usually an indication that the student didn't quite meet expectations during the regular school year. Like any other outside-the-mainstream program designed to help students keep up with their classes, it carries with it a stigma not only for the child, but also for the parent. Accepting the fact that your child needs extra help can be challenging. We want to believe that we don't care what anyone else thinks, but the reality is usually quite the opposite. The respect of our tribe is important to us. And a child not keeping up in school may translate into the assumption that the family is somehow lacking.

Facing the issue squarely and with compassion is a sign of parental maturity. Turning that challenge into positive gains requires a serious look at the reasons for the need. Does your child have difficulty learning? Have you allowed too many extracurricular activities to get in the way of academics? Does your child have trouble focusing? Has natural teen rebelliousness turned school into the enemy? Your ability to address such questions when your heart is aching for your child is one of the painful challenges of your job as Mom or Dad.

Of course, there is also the possibility that your child is attending summer school not out of need but purely for enrichment purposes. In that case, kudos. But remember that just as you can't shoulder all the blame when a child falls behind, you also can't take all the credit when he or she excels.

HAVE A FAMILY GAME NIGHT™

Forgive the designers of THE GAME OF LIFE board game for putting a little self-referential plug here. But regardless of the goal, there is wisdom in this space. Sitting around a table (NOT a computer or TV screen) playing a game with your family allows for a kind of bonding impossible elsewhere. No sports (except perhaps wrestling) can duplicate the proximity.

Plus, playing games speeds along the development of key skills. Don't think that because a game is based purely on the luck of dice or a spinner that your child isn't learning something. Playing board games encourages practical skills (adding dice, visualizing the move before actually making it). It shows that pleasure comes from trying hard to win within a set of rules. And it teaches how to win and how to lose.

A few tips for encouraging game play at home:

*Have games easily accessible. Putting them on a top shelf or hidden away in a closet renders them easily forgettable.

*Play whether your kids are part of the game or not. Just like seeing parents reading on a regular basis encourages kids to read, seeing parents playing games makes kids more likely to want a piece of the action.

*Don't discourage your kids from playing the same game over and over again. The familiarity of repetition is important.

*Avoid talks of winners and losers once the game has been put away.

LEARN SIGN LANGUAGE

Learning a second language is becoming increasingly important. But if you are interested in broadening your horizons, don't narrow your thinking to languages based on geography or ethnicity.

Here is the sign language alphabet:

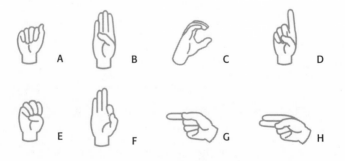

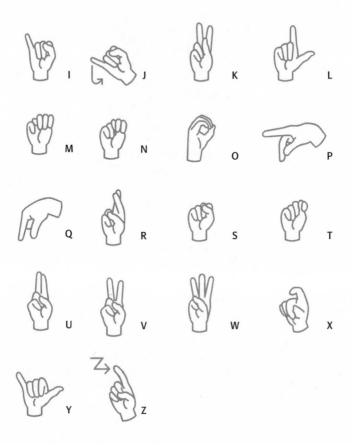

Wow. You've learned a whole new alphabet in just minutes. Maybe it's time to think about going back to school (see pages 61 and 95).

SPECIAL SECTION 3:

MORE LIFE QUOTES

"If life is a bowl of cherries, what am I doing in the pits?"
—Erma Bombeck

"I should have no objection to go over the same life from its beginning
to the end: requesting only the advantage authors have, of correcting in
a second edition the faults of the first."
—Benjamin Franklin

"Books are where things are explained to you; life is where things aren't."
—Julian Barnes

"Life is something to do when you can't get to sleep.
—Fran Liebowitz

"If A is a success in life, then A equals x plus y plus z. Work is x; y is play;
and z is keeping your mouth shut."
—Albert Einstein

"In the book of life, the answers aren't in the back."
—Charlie Brown (via Charles Schulz)

"Life is like playing a violin solo in public and learning the instrument as one goes on."
—Samuel Butler

"Life must be understood backwards, but it must be lived forward."
—Soren Kirkegaard.

"I love living. I have some problems with my life, but living is the best thing they've come up with so far."
—Neil Simon, from his play *The Last of the Red Hot Lovers.*

"I have set before you life and death, blessing and cursing: therefore choose life, that both thou and thy seed may live"
—Deuteronomy

"A great way to find out what you want from life is to write your own epitaph."
—Libbie Fudim

"A life of frustration is inevitable for any coach whose main enjoyment is winning."
—Chuck Noll

"A man has the right to toot his own horn to his heart's content, so long as he stays in his own home, keeps his windows closed and does not make himself obnoxious to his neighbors."
—Tioro

"A man must be strong enough to mold the peculiarity of his imperfections into the perfection of his peculiarities."
—Walter Rathena

BUY LAKESIDE CABIN
Pay
$90,000

You've worked hard, have money in the bank, and now you have decided that one home is not enough. Bully for you. Now where is it going to be?

You may want a change of pace and a change of place. If you are living in the city, think country. Living rural? Then think urban. Ask yourself what opportunities you want a new place to offer that you don't have right now.

Also consider the time you really want to spend there and the time it will take you to get to your new front door. Your thoughts may pull you toward a condo by a ski resort. But if the two flights and a rented car ride means you only get there once or twice a season, you have to ask yourself whether you aren't just better off renting. And if the vacation home is just an hour or two drive away, you have to wonder if you will really be able to leave your troubles at home.

Be warned that if you are buying a second home in a vacation area, it's very likely that you'll suddenly find yourself very popular with family and friends looking to visit. If that's one of the reasons you bought the place, great. Even so, you should be clear on house rules. Don't be afraid to say no to Cousin Ralph and his family. Remember that you do not have to spend every waking moment entertaining.

BURGLAR!
Pay
$50,000
if not insured

Just about anything a burglar might steal from your house is replaceable. The cash. The TV. Even the jewelry.

What is more difficult to recover is your sense of security. Your home—an extension of you—has been violated. Your turf has been encroached upon. Your sense of comfort destroyed. Reality: We live in a world that can be divided into two groups. There are those that have more than you and those that have less than you. Within both of those groups are subsets of people who want to increase what they have by taking it away from others. Some do this through legal channels, some don't. While THE GAME OF LIFE board is peppered with spaces that damage your money supply, this is a rare case of one where another human being causes your distress.

After being robbed, there is a healing process to go through. Know that it may take you a while to feel comfortable again in your own house. If an added security system helps that process, by all means go for it. If you look askance at strangers, acknowledge to yourself the reason for it. Like healing from a car accident (see page 56) or moving on after a death, it is absurd to expect normalcy overnight.

WIN NOBEL PRIZE
Collect
$100,000

Okay, so the makers of most board games get a little carried away some-times. In Careers®, for example, there's the opportunity to go to Mars (in early editions, it was the moon). In Monopoly® there's a chance to buy the Electric Company. And here, in THE GAME OF LIFE board game, play-ers get to join the ranks of the top-of-the-tops in their fields.

So let's buy into it and take a look at the kind of company you are keeping. Some of the Nobel Prize categories are packed with past win-ners whose names you might know.

In literature the award has been given to, among others, Rudyard Kipling, George Bernard Shaw, Sinclair Lewis, Eugene O'Neill, Pearl S. Buck, William Faulkner, John Steinbeck, Jean-Paul Sartre, Alexander Solzhenitsyn, and Isaac Bashevis Singer.

For the peace prize, there's a who's who in world history, including Nelson Mandela, the Dalai Lama, Elie Wiesel, Albert Schweitzer and Theodore Roosevelt.

What does it mean that you are unlikely to find a household name in the other categories? You have to go back to Enrico Fermi in 1938 to find one in physics. In chemistry, you might keep searching until 1911 where you'll find Marie Curie, nee Sklodowska. It's highly possible that you won't recognize anyone in medicine. Economics was added in 1968, so the history isn't quite as deep as the other categories, but still, you wouldn't be able to pick these guys out of a line-up.

Spin this negatively and you could conclude that we don't properly celebrate the people who change the world for the better.

Spin it positively, though, and you can use this as a reminder that it is futile to make fame your top priority. You can influence the lives of people all over the planet and still be unknown. You could make the world more livable or even keep its people from destroying it and still not be stopped by an autograph-seeker. Much of what is good about the world is good because of people whose names you'll never know. Remember that the next time you have the opportunity to hold a door open for someone behind you.

BUY HOME GYM
Pay
$30,000

If you find yourself not getting to the gym enough (you were warned about picking one too far away from home back on page 113), then perhaps it's time to invest in some home gym equipment. The options are impossibly wide—ranging from tiny devices that infomercial spokespeople claim can work ab-miracles to extensive fancy apparati that could fill an apartment.

Once you figure out how much space you have to devote to body betterment, then it's time to do some serious shopping. Beware of products you see on TV. It's better, of course, to try the pieces out yourself. If you want to avoid having just another place to hang your laundry, then be realistic about what the machine can do and what you can do.

Don't expect miracles. One machine will not make you look like a cover boy for *Men's Health* magazine, or one of the tennis-playing Williams sisters. Without a reasonable diet, exercise can only do so much. Focusing only on exercise is like being a company with a great manufacturing unit, but a lousy shipping and receiving department.

Assuming your health allows, it is wise to think about both cardiovascular activity and muscle strengthening/toning. A treadmill, stair stepper, stationery bike, and the like can fulfill the pulse-elevating portion of the work out. Anything from hand weights to a top of the line total body gym can do the toning trick. And, for your abs, don't underestimate the power of good old-fashioned crunches. Remember: people were in better shape when they actually got out and did stuff. Stay active.

STOCK MARKET CRASH 2

It's down again. But by now you should be getting used to it.

By this time, you should understand the market a little better and have some idea of where your money is best served. The next time the stock rises, it could be the time to cash out and start making disbursements to your children (the better to circumvent high inheritance taxes), or to shift some money into a college fund or to finally visit the Grand Canyon (see page 148).

TORNADO TILTS HOUSE!
Pay
$125,000
if not insured

Disaster again, this time in the form of the funnel cloud made so popular in the movies *The Wizard of Oz* and, sixty years later, *Twister*.

The unique thing about a tornado is that, unlike a hurricane, it can be grasped by the eye. You can see it coming. Its bottom skids across the ground seemingly uncertain about the path to take. When it hits, though, there is no fighting it.

In life, there are problems that we can see coming. There are battles that we know are on the horizon but that we cannot and should not fight. In such cases, the best strategy is to collect what is important and get out of danger's path. Standing and fighting serves no purpose but to increase risk. Yes, this force will destroy your house, but you will survive if you can summon the courage to get out in time.

MOO-SHU FLU ATTACK!/
LIFE-SAVING OPERATION
Pay
$25,000

Not quite sure how the Moo-Shu flu attack ended up on THE GAME OF LIFE board and, frankly, don't want to know.

So let's move on to the space that replaced it.

It seems like there's been a major curve ball thrown on the otherwise mostly blissful board. It's one thing to face the financial difficulties of a stock market plunge or a tornado-destroyed house, it's another to face the fact that you may not have a tomorrow. This one isn't just an operation—it's a life-saving operation. And that's got to make you rethink your priorities. You'll notice how in the next two spaces you're buying a sailboat and sponsoring a golf tournament. Clearly you've been motivated to treat yourself and to be charitable. But what are the long-term effects of a near-death experience? Does it prod you to explore your religious beliefs in more depth? Does it lead you to spend more time with family and close friends? Do you find yourself not getting as stressed about what now are clearly small things? Or do you revert to your former self, as if the operation were no more significant than a root canal.

Denial, after all, is a powerful drug. We need a bit of it or else we would be too terrified to cross the street. But too much of it and we have no incentive to take advantage of every day we are given.

BUY SAILBOAT
Pay
$30,000

While sailboats may have been one of the earliest forms of water transportation, they aren't used much anymore for getting from one place to the other. Usually, the dock of departure for a sailboat is the same as the dock of arrival. Owners of boats "take them out" as if they were dogs that needed walking.

Purchasing a sailboat can do as much damage to your wallet as purchasing a car, but this is clearly a luxury. Unless you are Gilligan or the Skipper, you can't count it as a necessity. (And if you are Gilligan or the Skipper, please make sure you have a functioning radio before you take off on a three-hour cruise.)

A sailboat also differs from a car in that you are expected to name it. This puts enormous pressure on you to be creative (making it, unless you are a pretentious estate-owner, the only non-living thing you are likely to ever name). Be careful not to celebrate one family member so as not to risk insulting another. Don't saddle it with the nickname that you've only had for a few months.

Unlike a car, it's easy to let a sailboat go without use. After all, your busy life doesn't allow you to take it out every week. Maybe not even every two. But let it go a couple of weeks in season and you'll be struck with the feeling that maybe this was an unwise purchase, like the toy you begged your parents for that proved to be not all that much fun once you took it out of the box.

SPONSOR GOLF TOURNAMENT
Pay
$35,000

As a kid, it's difficult to imagine a game of golf without a windmill to hit the ball through or a free game for landing the ball in a shark's mouth on the 18th hole.

But soon you realize that there's a golf game that involves more than just a putter. Maybe you give it a try. You'll either see it as a great game of concentration, skill, and practice, or, in the words of Mark

Twain, "a good walk, spoiled."

Whichever way you go, there's no denying that golf tournaments are right up there with silent auctions as prime tools of charity fundraisers. And so you throw yourself into the fray, trying to attract an impressive lineup of local athletes, business leaders, politicians, and TV anchors to join the foursomes.

There's a reason why golf has as much a reputation for business schmoozing as it does for showing off athletic skills. Being involved in such activities puts you in the proximity of people of power. Play tennis and you may have a little time before and after the set to talk, but golf gives you the strolling time, the chance to watch your opponent, the opportunity to see how he or she handles pressure. But while you may be playing against someone, you are also playing with the person as part of a foursome. By the 18th hole, you've gotten through a battle together.

MID-LIFE CRISIS
START NEW CAREER

Every life has regrets. What would have happened if you had gone to medical school instead of working toward an engineering degree? Would you still be the same person if you had hitchhiked across Europe, as you planned to do in college? What if you had been a little more polite to the plainclothes officer at the bar that night?

It's natural, therefore, to periodically assess what you've done and where you are going. This reaches the level of crisis when it throws into turmoil those you love and all you have worked so hard to achieve. When you hit such a point—whether it occurs mid-life, in your mid-30s or mid-semester—try to understand what you are rejecting from your life, and be careful not to risk the rest. Remember that a change of career may be just the thing—contrary to what you may think after seeing Mariah Carey act or hearing Bruce Willis sing.

Okay, so many a lawyer who thought he was the next John Grisham found himself instead becoming the next Moe Hildalgo (no, never heard of him either). But it's just that lack of a guarantee that makes a career change exciting.

8

MILLIONAIRE ESTATES

PRODUCE ROCK VIDEO/
HOST ONLINE CONCERT
Pay
$100,000

The latest version of our favorite board game changed "Produce Rock Video" to "Host Online Concert," an attempt to catch the Internet music wave. Either way, you're becoming a part of the rock scene without needing to demonstrate any musical talent.

The Game of Life

Being part of a rock band is a common fantasy. But by the time you've reached this space on the board, you probably are too old to break into the market (Quick: Name a single rock entertainer who appeared on the national radar after age 35?). Accepting the fantasies you'll never fulfill is one of the bittersweet parts of growing up.

Still, you are apparently now in the music biz. Will your video be one that reaches MTV or VH1 and becomes the visual track that runs in fans' minds whenever they hear the song on the radio? Or will it collect dust with the thousands of others that are made with cash and dreams in an effort to launch just about every garage band in America? A better question, at least to those readers who came of age after the video revolution, is: How does being given a visual representation of music effect our ability to enjoy music purely as music?

To be sure, pop music has always had a visual component. One could argue for days about whether Elvis or The Beatles could have reached the heights of success they reached without television and magazines to take their pictures to the masses. But would we accept a performer even if we did not have a visual representation of that person?

That is not to say that all popular performers need to fit into the same mold. Certainly Meatloaf, Mama Cass, and Ozzie Osbourne don't fit into any central-casting concept of "pop star," but there is no denying that each one's "look" contributed to their popularity.

We do get that one chance to judge purely on the aural—when we hear an unknown song on the radio from a performer we've never heard before. As we smile or catch the groove and hum along, or just listen and wait after the song for the deejay to clue us in, we experience the one-of-a-kind sensation of pure music pleasure. As long as you aren't the one driving, just close your eyes and enjoy.

HELP THE HOMELESS

Feel guilty every time you walk past a panhandler without dropping change into his hand? Don't want to drop those coins because of the likelihood that the money will go to alcohol or drugs?

A quick way to solve this conflict: When you are facing the choice of whether or not to give money to someone on the street, take the money you would give and put it in another pocket. When that money reaches a critical mass (just walk through a big city and that won't take long), donate that money to a legitimate agency that actually helps the homeless and doesn't contribute to the problem.

Otherwise, you are simply appeasing your guilt by giving to the most vocal and aggressive of the homeless (who may not actually be home-less) and ignoring the many homeless who are actually struggling to better their lives. Shelters and networks exist that are trying to help people get back on their feet. You don't have to offer just your dollars though. Your time can be just as valuable to those who are in need of help (see page 99). Can there be a better feeling than knowing that the time you put in didn't just feed a person a meal, but helped him get on his feet again?

HAVE TATTOOS REMOVED/
HAVE COSMETIC SURGERY
Pay
$100,000

What once was a tattoo space on the board has been replaced with one dealing with cosmetic surgery. Both involve the rethinking of one's looks. In the case of cosmetic surgery, it is generally done in an attempt to remake your self. The results can range from embarrassing to jaw-dropping. Before considering such an expenditure, though, you should seriously consider your reasons. You should also understand clearly what you hope to get out of it, physically and emotionally. Has the shape of your nose always bothered you, or only since you've noticed younger people getting attention from those who used to eyeball you? Is that flab the natural result of aging, or have you neglected exercise and spent too much time in the fast-food drive-thru lane?

As for tattoos, this space isn't about joining the now very mainstream trend, but about removing one. Apparently you've come to realize that way back when you didn't know everything. Still, even with "I told you so" being tossed at you by parents, siblings, or friends, it's important to realize that no one was really harmed by your choice. Yes, the removal is costly and uncomfortable. But so what? If all goes reasonably well, you'll reach a point in life when you accept that the mistakes you made weren't big, big mistakes. And even if you made one or two doozies, you should realize that repair or correction is possible.

To decide that your mistakes have made you irreparable is to accept that life is, for most intents and purposes, over. You are now just marking time. On the other hand, to see that you have reached today and that it's up to you to decide what pieces of yourself you are carrying forward to tomorrow, is a sign that you understand Bob Dylan's line that, "He who is not busy being born is busy dying."

Continue to be born.

COLLEGE

Pay

$5000
per child

You've heard horror stories about the soaring cost of college education—but no matter how well you prepare, there's a good chance you won't be ready for this. Four years of a state college—tuition and fees only—is estimated at over $60,000 for a student entering in 2020. Let's not even talk about the Ivy League. Maybe the $5,000 fee here is just for the books.

Putting the cost aside, though, there are issues to face when your child is ready for college. One of the things you have to deal with as an adult—which you never really thought about as a teen—is that you are paying for your child to attend a school that you haven't chosen. When you were arguing with your parents about where you were going, it didn't seem like such a big deal—of course you would go where you wanted to go. This was your life.

But now it's difficult to imagine why your child isn't taking your sage advice. Surely you are being practical. Surely you have his best interest in mind. Surely she can see that.

This is a time when tempers can flair. And a big part of that can be blamed on your subconscious realization that you are soon going to be saying goodbye, knowing that you are no longer in control of your baby's day-to-day life. You will no longer be the touchstone at the end of the day. Remember how much of a wreck you were waiting in the living room when she was two hours late? Now imagine going weeks without knowing what she's wearing, what she's eating, and who she's dating.

So dive into the book you've been wanting to read. Take the trip you've wanted to take. And when the phone doesn't ring, try to remember what it was like to be 18 and suddenly part of a much bigger world, rather than 50 and feeling suddenly part of a much smaller one.

VISIT WAR MEMORIAL

If you didn't serve in the military, it may take you the better part of a lifetime to fully appreciate the sacrifices made by those who enlisted or were drafted into the armed forces. Until then, these monuments may seem as distant as Stonehenge. Signs of a people so impossible to understand that even trying to comprehend them seems futile.

By now, you have no doubt realized that life is precious. You've fallen in love, held a child, experienced the death of someone close to you. The maturation of that understanding makes one even more awestruck by the sacrifices of the military.

Saving Private Ryan woke a lot of people up to the sacrifices demanded at times of war. September 11th, 2001 further reminded us of our vulnerability. We live in a complicated world and a complicated time. Sometimes lines are drawn and lines are crossed and things that are fundamental to our understanding of life are violated. Tough decisions are made. People die as a result of those decisions.

When time has done some of its work, we build these places of remembrance. As you face challenges in your civilian life, a visit to one of these places can help give you perspective, new insight into how to face life's seemingly impossible challenges, and a greater appreciation for the freedom that's been won for you.

SPONSOR ART EXHIBIT
Pay
$125,000

A number of spaces back, you participated in an art auction. Then you gave to an art museum. But buying art and giving a donation don't carry the weight of sponsorship. So here you go sponsoring an art exhibit.

Being a sponsor isn't as easy as it may sound, though. Whatever you endorse with your wallet will come to represent you. If your name is attached to something that the public objects to or that some patrons find offensive, then you may be held as responsible as the artist. Yet if you object to something a curator wants in the exhibit, you risk coming across as narrow-minded and meddlesome.

So why should you put your money into an organization without having any say as to how it is spent? On the other hand, if patrons are given veto power, then the decision-making leaves the hands of trained curators and could fall into the hands of dilettantes (no offense).

Being wealthy—and if you're sponsoring an art exhibition, there's a good chance you are—carries with it such dilemmas. It takes a strong person to know whether his or her opinions are being considered because they are worth considering or because the listener is afraid that the purse will be closed.

The alternative, though, is to leave culture to the whim of government funding and/or the marketplace. Museums, theater companies, and ballet troupes will never be able to pay for themselves through ticket sales. Making them part of your philanthropy points to an understanding that mankind needs roses in addition to bread

GRAND CANYON VACATION

One of the most awe-inspiring aspects of the Grand Canyon is the sheer amount of empty space we see between "Here" and "There."

It's highly possible that you'll never be so aware of the space between things as you are when looking across the work that this river has done. Most of us have seen mountains. We've seen earth cutting dramatically into sky. But here it feels like sky cutting into earth. It can be seen from space, this massive gash in the Earth, and it reminds us explicitly of the effect that time will have on everything we know. Our planet is patient it seems from looking down from the rim, but it is also persistent. It clearly will get what it wants eventually.

A Grand Canyon vacation is not fully complete without a short drive west to the Hoover Dam. Here, the powerful natural vistas of river and rock are garnished with a slab of man's handiwork. Here, the force of the river is stopped and regulated by a wall and the impression is both empowering and humbling. It is an engineering wonder and enormous in scope, but it is still dwarfed by the seemingly endless landscape.

The one-two combination of The Grand Canyon and The Hoover Dam is unparalleled anywhere. To travel to other continents in search of wonders without having seen these seems almost un-American. Go ahead and make the trip. It will renew your faith in nature and humankind.

GO FISHING

Stand-up comic Ron Gallup said that fishing is not a sport, it's a practical joke. Think about it: You are dangling what appears to be food in front of an unsuspecting victim. Then, when a bite is taken: Surprise! There's a metal hook imbedded in its cheek.

If you can get past that image, there is much to enjoy about fishing. It's a sport where the downtime can make the uptime worthwhile. It's that rare sport where conversation is possible, where success can come at any moment, where beer can be consumed while you are "playing," and where generations can play together on a relatively level playing field.

It's a sport that you can participate in all over the world and, for the most part, play by your own rules. You can play for as long a time as you like, bring along whomever you like, and take a nap if you want to.

It is, most importantly, a way to relax. No matter what point you are in your life, understand and absorb the importance of kicking back once in a while. Whether that's with a fishing pole in hand or not is really beside the point.

HIRE JOCKEY FOR YOUR RACEHORSE
Pay
$65,000

Owning a racehorse is an opportunity to be in a high-stakes, adrenaline-pumped athletic environment without actually breaking a sweat yourself—unless, of course, you've got your bankroll riding on the nose.

But like owning a football franchise, you are at the mercy of the talent you've assembled. You can hire the best jockey, focus all your energies on diet and exercise and training for both beast and rider, but from the moment they leave the starting gate, there is nothing you can do except cheer. Owning a racehorse—or even just putting a $2 bet on one—teaches us that, at some point, we have to accept the fact that there are monents in any business when things are at least temporarily out of our control.

GO HIKING!

How many natural corners of your state are there that you haven't visited?

To put a finer point on it, how many natural areas in your own town haven't you visited?

It is very easy, if you don't live in a place as visually spectacular as, say, Maui, to lament your town's shortcomings. But like L.A. residents who bemoan their city's lack of culture, it's really just a matter of making a slight effort to go out and find the natural beauty around you.

A hike isn't just an opportunity to experience visual splendor. It is also a time for contemplation—for one-foot-in-front-of-the-other philosophizing, for self-examination, and for sustained thought without advertisers vying for your attention. Like the God of Genesis taking a day of rest, this is an opportunity to assess the day, week, or whatever time period gone by and to anticipate the time ahead. It's a chance to take stock of what you've got and what you need to do. It's a deliberate moment of not working.

It's also very good exercise. If you hike enough, there's a good chance you'll end up with an awesome set of gams.

PLANT A TREE

A tree represents both roots to our past and branches to the future.

The act of planting—of putting something in the ground and watching it grow—indicates an understanding that you are part of an ongoing process on this planet. That after you've gone, the tree will keep going.

Grandparents, readers of science fiction, scientists, medical researchers, and historians understand this uniquely human ability to see past our tomorrows. While some people become obsessed with mortality—the fact that each of us will one day die—others embrace the miracle that others will live beyond us.

To take action now to make the world better for the future—time that could be spent furthering our own ends for this lifetime—is one of the great unselfish acts.

SUPPORT WILDLIFE FUND

We see animals at the zoo, perhaps keep a pet or two in the house, and once in a while stop to observe the flight of birds over our homes.

A few spaces back, you went on an African Safari (see page 104). Perhaps it was the sight of those real–life animals in their natural surroundings that inspired you to make a wildlife fund donation. Perhaps it was your kids, who tend to have a greater sensitivity to such things, who prodded you to write a check. Donating money to help keep alive a creature that would eat you if it had a chance may seem a foolish prospect. Understanding why the survival of one species in a world full of millions matters all that much isn't easy.

But instinctually most of us know that we share the planet. One can argue what the relationship between man and beast should be (and if you are or know a vegetarian or anti-fur activist, you've already had this discussion), but there's no denying that man has contributed to the extinction of many species. And these extinctions are as forever as the demise of the dinosaurs. Understanding the vulnerability of what is here right now can lead to a stronger spiritual connection to the world around you. And can help determine what will still be around for future generations.

TOUR EUROPE/
HAVE WEBSITE DESIGNED
Pay
$45,000

Touring is different than traveling. When you hopped a night bus from Chicago to LA, you were traveling. When you road tripped to Lauderdale for Spring Break, you were traveling. When you packed up the kids and drove five hours to Six Flags (and had to make seven stops) you were traveling.

When you sign on for a trip knowing that a guide will meet you at the airport, help you with your bags, escort you to an air-conditioned bus, get on the microphone, and share an historical anecdote for every street you pass, you are touring.

Travelers get lost. Tourists don't.

Travelers have to search for answers. Tourists ask their guide.

Travelers can return from a trip knowing nothing but their specific experience. Tourists get more info than they may want.

Travelers get a unique experience of a place. Tourists get a common experience of a place.

Travelers might miss "the good parts." Tourists might miss the surprising parts.

Forget specific vacations. Step back for a minute and ask yourself if you've gone through your life so far as a traveler or as a tourist.

If you are playing the most recent edition of THE GAME OF LIFE board game, you're bypassing the Europe trip and, instead, having a web site developed. So what does your personal stop on the information superhighway say about you? Is it a stop designed purely for friends and family? Is it an effort to present yourself to the outside world—to share your poetry or your photography or your stories without bothering with traditional publishing? Are you trying to lure others into a multi-level marketing scheme? Is it your opportunity to make clear how much you love your favorite celebrity?

The important thing is not to put too much of a stake in this little piece of cyber-real estate. Your real life, away from the screen, is what's important. The Internet is a tool that, if you use it right, can help you easily collect information, connect to people with similar interests, play a little backgammon, and perhaps do a little business. But it's nothing compared to the real world. And your website is not you.

YOU'RE A GRANDPARENT!

One of your babies has had a baby. And you get to hold it and play with it and make it smile and hand it back when it screams, pukes, or poops in its pants.

There are some things a grandparent should never forget:

*The most valuable thing you can give your grandchild is a memorable experience. If you are in a position to make even a small-scale family-gathering weekend happen, do it. And don't complain about it (at least, not in front of the grandchildren).

*Yes, you made some mistakes raising your own children. And your children will make some mistakes raising theirs. For everyone's sake, remember your own stumbles.

*Advise but don't dictate. Your child is raising a child in a different world than the one in which you raised yours. Choose your battles.

*If you do get into a disagreement with your grandchild's parents, hold the discussion until you are out of earshot of the little one's. Or until he or she is asleep. Either way, keep in mind the child is probably listening.

*If you can, seize the opportunity to have one-on-one time with each of your grandchildren. Many kids only get to experience their parents' parents when there are lots of people around. One-on-one time, whether it's a weekend getaway or an afternoon at the zoo, can lead to a wonderful relationship.

*Phone calls are great. E-mails are a technological wonder. But a letter in the mail is something special. And the dollar you put in is always appreciated.

PAY DAY 4

You've reached the last Pay Day on the board. From here on in, you've got a party, a cruise, pension, and retirement.

When you collect your first paycheck of your working life, it's difficult to believe that a day like this will actually come. In some way, you've been working for other people your entire life (unless you are an entrepreneur who never brought a partner into the fold and never took a company public, or unless you have been independently wealthy all of your life). You've entered into a contract, verbal or written, saying that you would perform a job and, in return, you would be paid.

Sounds simple, but when that relationship ends, so too does your dependence on pleasing someone else with your work. After you accept your final paycheck, you no longer have to convince anyone—including yourself—that the work you have done has been worth the compensation.

It can be a major burden, this self-reliance. It can be a challenge to accept that you are no longer part of a team, striving toward a common business goal. Retirement (see page 159) is just around the corner. But it starts when this check gets deposited into your checking account.

Let your final paycheck represent a career worth celebrating.

THROW PARTY FOR ENTERTAINMENT AWARD WINNERS
Pay
$35,000

The older GAME OF LIFE boards announce that you've somehow gotten into the position of throwing a party for Grammy-award winners. It's since been modified to mere "entertainment award" winners. Either way, it's a space nearly as improbable as winning a Nobel Prize (see page 132). Rather than throwing a party for music industry bigwigs, you'll be more likely throw a party for your friends to *watch* the Grammy's.

Watching the awards, you may be—like about-to-retire people since music was created—wondering aloud why today's tunes aren't as good as they were when you were young. Popular music has always been a right-age-at-the-right-time phenomenon. Growing older means accepting that most of the music on the radio is not intended for you. It can be rough to face the fact that pop culture marketers are no longer targeting your generation. For a reality check, take a look at the top ten songs for whatever year you consider the peak of your musical connectiveness.

No doubt half the songs are just plain silly, whether you're of the era of "Leader of the Pack," "Seasons in the Sun," or "Achy Breaky Heart." What seemed right to you in 19-whatever may mean nothing to the kids today. That's because they weren't you and the songs didn't come on the radio at just the right time in their lives.

LUXURY CRUISE/
INVEST IN E-COMMERCE COMPANY
Pay
$55,000

If you could have on your bookshelf, a volume dedicated to your family's story, chances are there would be a section devoted to an ocean voyage. That might have been a trip on the Mayflower. It might have scenes taking place on the crowded deck of an immigrant ship. It may have been a state-of-the-art luxury craft bringing your ancestors over to the new world in style. Or it may involve your great-greats and great-great-greats in shackles on a slave ship.

These days, if you take a trip by ship, you are a lot less likely to be relocating and more likely to be recreating. These massive boats are outfitted for pleasure, loading up passengers with any-time-of-day buffets, non-stop activity, plenty of reclining chairs for those who don't want to take advantage of non-stop activity, and a smiling staff eager to serve.

But the lure of the sea remains, even if you spend more time in the on-deck pool then you do looking out at the vast ocean. This time, look out over the deck and take in the view you won't get anywhere else. Take a moment and honor your ancestors' bravery—whether they came voluntarily or not—by imagining the not knowing, the anxiety, the hope, and the fear that they faced entering a new world. Try to compare even the toughest challenges you've faced to what they faced both in route and once they arrived.

If you are playing the updated version, you're investing in an e-commerce company. Boy, did you arrive late. Let this space show you how even THE GAME OF LIFE board game can't keep up with the fast-pace changes in real life.

PENSION
Collect
$20,000
times spin

The very notion of a pension seems an impossibility in this job-hopping world. Unlike in your grandparents' day, even the most loyal contemporary worker is unlikely to spend a working lifetime with one company. The days of gold-watch-rewards for stick-aroundness are fading away, and with them the identification of person with company. Way back when, you thought you had so much time to save for this day, but here it is, and the pension ain't what you hoped it would be.

For celebrators of the individual, this seems like a good thing. Why should you go through your entire life seeing yourself as a GE employee or part of the Ford team when the higher-ups at the company don't know you from anyone else on the factory floor? "Our lives are more than our work," says one activist folksong, "And our work is more than our jobs."

There's a sadness to it, though, this fluidness. Just as it is more diffi-cult to root for a baseball team that makes major trades every season, it's difficult to feel a bond with a company when you know that your co-workers, and you, are likely to have moved on to other pastures in five years' time. And when you can't form a bond, it's harder to be as productive as you might otherwise have been. This puts you at risk, increasing the chance that you'll move on (whether by your choice or your bosses) thus perpetuating the problem.

RETIRE

Career paths come to an end. That may sound appealing when you are young, but as the fateful day approaches you can't help but feel ambiva-lent. What will you do? After years of working for other people, can you hold up to the pressure of designing your own day? Can you tolerate being around your significant other 24/7?

Surely, that choice doesn't present itself so clearly for some. For many workers, retirement simply means being required to leave a career job and, without the financial means to continue as is, find another place of employment.

For others, it's the reward for a lifetime of work well done. If you have a healthy relationship it's a chance to spend time with the spouse who has stuck with you all these years. A chance to visit grandkids, to repair a garden, to crack the books you've been putting off. To sleep in. To reconnect with friends. To travel to far-off exotic places. To contemplate a life well lived...so far. You still may well have 40 years to go! Enjoy them.

COUNTRYSIDE ACRES
AND MILLIONAIRE ESTATES

If you are playing THE GAME OF LIFE board game, this is the time to add up your money and use that as a gauge of how successful you've been. But in life, there is no such moment.

While there is no predetermined time to do this kind of life assessment, there is also no bad time to do it. Taking a serious look at your accomplishments, shortcomings, high points and lows, you are declaring this moment, right now, as the starting point for change. Seen this way, today becomes a launching point from which to take the good from the past and learn from the rest.

Even if real life brings you to Millionaire Estates—even if you find yourself with the most money, the most positive life experiences, the most kids and the best home—there is still an adventure ahead of you. There are still places to go and books to read and people to encounter and learn from. There are still people to help and challenges to face and horizons to be drawn toward.

Unlike playing a board game, you've got one shot at life.

Make the most of it every day.

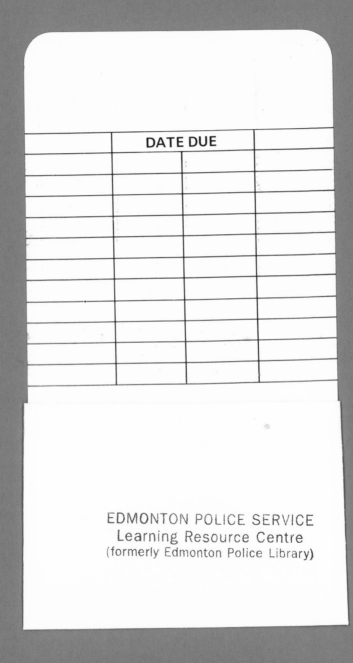

DATE DUE